Wilderness Time

Other RENOVARÉ Resources for Spiritual Renewal

Devotional Classics
co-edited by Richard J. Foster
and James Bryan Smith

Embracing the Love of God
by James Bryan Smith

Songs for Renewal
by Janet Lindeblad Janzen
with Richard J. Foster

A Spiritual Formation Journal
created by Jana Rea
with Richard J. Foster

A Spiritual Formation Workbook
by James Bryan Smith

Wilderness Time

A Guide to Spiritual Retreat

Emilie Griffin

A RENOVARÉ Resource for Spiritual Renewal

HarperSanFrancisco
An Imprint of HarperCollinsPublishers

For information about RENOVARÉ, write to RENOVARÉ,
8 Inverness Drive East, Suite 102, Englewood, CO
80112–5609.

HarperCollins Web Site: http://www.harpercollins.com
HarperCollins,® ♣,® and HarperSanFrancisco™ are trade-
marks of HarperCollins Publishers Inc.

FIRST EDITION

Library of Congress Cataloging-in-Publication Data
Griffin, Emilie.
Wilderness time : a guide to spiritual retreat / Emilie
Griffin.
1st ed.
Includes bibliographical references
ISBN 0–06–063361–1 (pbk.)
1. Retreats—Christianity. I. Title.
BV5068.R4G74   1997   269'.6—dc21   97–615

97 98 99 00 01 ❖ RRDH 10 9 8 7 6 5 4 3

For Sister Janet Franklin, CSJ,
dear friend and companion in the experience
of creative retreat.

Contents

Foreword

I rejoice in *Wilderness Time*. It is an invitation to retreat that truly invites. It welcomes me, entreats me, draws me into "the country of God's affections," as Emilie Griffin puts it.

It invites, first of all, because its author is writing from lived experience. She has taken retreat not just once, or now and again, but as a firm pattern of life. And she does this out of the context of the busy, pressured life of an advertising executive, first in New York City and now in New Orleans. Just like you and me, Emilie Griffin has telephone calls to return, letters to write, bills to pay, family obligations to meet. And still she finds place and space for retreat . . . or perhaps it is *because* of these persistent demands that she finds place and space for retreat. This is a genuine encouragement to me. You see, I want to learn about retreat from people who know what it feels like to have unwieldy "to do" lists endlessly vying for their time and attention.

Wilderness Time also invites because it is doable. No spiritual heroics here. It takes me by the hand and shows me how I can actually integrate this way of living into *my* life and *my* schedule. It is not that it pampers my obsession with much-ness and manyness. To the contrary. Ms. Griffin writes, "When there is no time to do it, that's when you most need to unclut-ter the calendar and go apart to pray. When the gridlock of your schedule relentlessly forbids it is the time you most need retreat." These words "speak truth to power" into me espe-cially when I am tempted to justify my inability to enter retreat by appeals to "the many demands placed upon me by others." No, the quality, the doability, is of a different sort. It is the sim-plicity. It is the earthiness. It is the bridge it builds from the Great Ages of Prayer to my world of computer icons and sound bites and Pop-Tarts. After reading this book I say, "Yes, I see. I understand. It is all one reality, this prayer and nursing babies, this solitude and business appointments, this spiritual discipline and ballet lessons."

Then, too, it invites by encouraging me to follow "the lead-ing-strings of God's grace." I like that. Oh, there are plenty of practical suggestions here. It even gives guidance for one-day, three-day, and seven-day retreats. But this is no "five steps to blessedness" manual. Emilie Griffin knows well the unpre-dictable nature of retreat. Regardless of how much we may plan our retreat—and there are generous planning ideas here—God is in charge of the retreat experience and we are not. This reality Emilie calls "God's improvisations." She writes, "You can never fully anticipate God's gifts to you in the retreat. . . . There is no way to orchestrate the black-eyed Susans growing wild in the path as you turn the corner with your Bible in hand."

And finally, it invites me because it calls me home. Home to peace and serenity and affirmation. Home to hope and friendship and openness. Home to acceptance and intimacy and joy. Home, home to God. It is as if buried deep in the human heart is a long-forgotten dream of "the beloved country" and *Wilderness Time* is calling me to remember once again. And so, I do.

Richard J. Foster
23 October 1996

CHAPTER 1

An Invitation

Times come when we yearn for more of God than our schedules will allow. We are tired, we are crushed, we are crowded by friends and acquaintances, commitments and obligations. The life of grace is abounding, but we are too busy for it! Even good obligations begin to hem us in.

Madeleine L'Engle writes: "Every so often I need OUT; something will throw me into total disproportion, and I have to get away from everybody—away from all those people I love most in the world—in order to regain a sense of proportion."[1]

Often, she says, she needs to get away completely, to her special place, a small brook in a green glade.

Like her, we wish for the kind of freedom we had as children, a carefree spirit, a jubilant heart. Refreshment is what we're after: playfulness, simplicity, a clear space, a time in the wilderness. In Hosea we read:

> Therefore, I will now allure her,
>   and bring her into the wilderness,
>   and speak tenderly to her,

From there I will give her her vineyards,
    and make the Valley of Achor a door of hope.
There she shall respond as in the days of her youth,
as at the time when she came out of the land of Egypt.
    (Hos. 2:14–15)

A separate time with God has powerful appeal. We long for time in the open with wildflowers blowing and blue sky stretching overhead, with birds calling and green trees sighing. We may wonder, is such a gifted time stored up for us anywhere?

In the country of God's affections, such a time and space are ours for the asking. God is waiting for us, expecting us, offering us a time of restoration. What we're looking for goes by the simple name: *retreat.*

There may, however, be something in us that resists or holds back from the experience of retreat. We may schedule the retreat, and then balk at it or stall in some way. These fearful, self-deceiving impulses are what sometimes keep us from prayer; we need to break away from such constraints and begin.

Spiritual formation involves a fundamental choice. Choosing to live for Jesus Christ may mean adopting a certain style of life or, perhaps more properly, a rule of life. We take on a series of spiritual practices that will open us to God's work in our lives.

This choice leads to dialogue with God; it warms our hearts for friendship with him.[2] Retreat offers the chance for a fresh start in the spiritual life. No doubt, if you are ready to make a retreat, you have made such a start once before, possibly more than once.

This need to begin and begin again is universal; it is basic to the disciplined life. In his sermon entitled "Christian Repentance," John Henry Newman writes, "The most perfect Christian is to himself but a beginner, a penitent prodigal, who has squandered God's gifts. . . . "[3]

Perseverance is needed to live out our fundamental commitment: to serve God, not randomly but over the long run. Not unlike a marriage or a religious vocation, this way of life is transforming; it *will* change us. Over and over we must make clean breaks, fresh starts, and new beginnings.

The philosopher Søren Kierkegaard wrote a long treatise titled *Purity of Heart Is to Will One Thing.* His notion of single-heartedness is a clue to the decisive nature of the spiritual life. To will one thing is to will over and over, beginning again and again, cutting loose from our past selves and stepping into the new drama of self-giving that is the disciplined life. Closer in time to us, the pastor and writer Eugene Peterson has written a book with a title that is a splendid metaphor of the spiritual life: *A Long Obedience in the Same Direction.*

As Paul the Apostle has it, we are running a race. We are taking on a kind of training that will shape us into the image of Christ. Retreat, which could be called a decisive moment extended in time, offers us a great opportunity to seek this kind of formation. We are choosing a specific opportunity for grace, a disciplined way that will give us direction. Yet this choice is realistic, not so outrageous or mock-heroic that we can't accomplish it. Retreat is a generous commitment to friendship with God: one that, despite false starts, stumbling, and all the different aspects of our humanity, will nevertheless act, by grace, to form us in Jesus Christ.

Retreat is an opportunity for spiritual formation in the style of Hebrews 12:

And you have forgotten the exhortation that addresses
you as children—

> "My child, do not regard lightly the discipline of the
>   Lord, or lose heart when you are punished by him;
> for the Lord disciplines those whom he loves,
>   and chastises every child whom he accepts."

Endure trials for the sake of discipline. God is treating
you as children; for what child is there whom a parent
does not discipline? If you do not have that discipline in
which all children share, then you are illegitimate and
not his children. Moreover, we had human parents to
discipline us, and we respected them. Should we not be
even more willing to be subject to the Father of spirits
and live? For they disciplined us for a short time as
seemed best to them, but he disciplines us for our good,
in order that we may share his holiness. Now, discipline
always seems painful rather than pleasant at the time,
but later it yields the peaceful fruit of righteousness to
those who have been trained by it.

Therefore lift your drooping hands and strengthen
your weak knees, and make straight paths for your feet,
so that what is lame may not be put out of joint, but
rather be healed. (Heb. 5–13)

Here we must apply our understanding that our God is a
loving father who wills our formation and our transformation
in an eager way. He is like the human father tenderly watching his young child take her first steps, then grab onto the side
of the sofa, then take another adventurous step, then sud-

denly sit down hard. Have you ever watched a baby learning to walk? Or a young bird learning to fly? The mother and father can't do it for the child. The child has to learn by taking chances, gaining balance, swaying. When you learn to walk, your parent is training you, egging you on, then reproaching and correcting, moving ahead of you on the path to show you how it's done.

Let's look again at those words in the Letter to the Hebrews, this time in a contemporary paraphrase by Eugene Peterson. Peterson's version jumps over some of the difficulties of culture that existed in earlier translations (like our discomfort with physical punishment of children and adults) and lays open the plain spiritual sense of the original:

> Or have you forgotten how good parents treat good children, and that God regards you as his children?
>
> "My dear child, don't shrug off God's discipline,
>   but don't be crushed by it either.
> It's the child he loves that he disciplines;
>   the child he embraces, he also corrects."
>
> God is educating you; that's why you must never drop out. He's treating you as dear children. This trouble you're in isn't punishment, it's *training,* the normal experience of children. Only irresponsible parents leave children to fend for themselves. Would you prefer an irresponsible God? We respect our own parents for training and not spoiling us, so why not embrace God's training so we can truly *live?* While we were children, our parents did what *seemed* best to them. But God is doing what *is* best for us, training us to live God's holy best.

At the time, discipline isn't much fun. It always feels like
it's going against the grain. Later, of course, it pays off
handsomely, for it's the well-trained who find themselves mature in their relationship with God.

So don't sit around on your hands! No more drag-
ging your feet! Clear the path for long-distance runners
so no one will trip and fall, so no one will step in a hole
and sprain an ankle. Help each other out. And run for it![4]

Think of the spiritual life as a pattern, a series of concrete
actions that will gently move us toward transformation in
Christ. The disciplines themselves, however, are not transformative. The transformation in us is God's work. It is a work of
grace.

That deeply transformative grace comes to us not through
our own doing but as pure gift. And yet something is demanded from us: the free gift of ourselves, our submission to
the gentle rod of Christian discipline, our willingness to be
transformed, our yielding to the grace of God. In the end our
yes is what's required. We have to say, "Speak, Lord, your servant is listening." We have to say, "Be it done to me according
to your will."

Is it hard to set aside time for retreat? Sometimes it seems
impossible. Yet how many hours, even days, do we spend in
the company of tiresome people, people who wear us down?
How much time do we spend searching for effectiveness? For
ways to manage our time? How much time do we spend worrying about things beyond our control?

Jesus deals with this overconcern. "And can any of you by
worrying add a single hour to your span of life? If then you are

not able to do so small a thing as that, why do you worry about the rest?" (Luke 12:25–26).

Finding time for retreat is as difficult as finding time for prayer in an ordinary, overscheduled day. Whether the time be days or minutes, the issues are the same. Is retreat one of our priorities? Does God have a place in our scheme? How far we have allowed ourselves to slide! How distant we feel from the spirit of prayer! Possibly the barrier is not time at all. What we are up against is not really the pressure of events, not the many demands on our time, but a stubbornness within ourselves, a hard-heartedness that will not yield to transformation and change.

Setting aside a morning, a day, even a week or more for spiritual retreat is one of the most strengthening and reinforcing experiences of our lives. We need to yield. We have to bend. Once we embrace the spiritual disciplines, we are carried along, often, by a storm of grace. Giving way to the power of spiritual disciplines becomes a step toward freedom, a movement into the wide-open spaces of the sons and daughters of God.

Retreat—with all of its prayerful beginnings and renewals—can become a step into reality. On retreat we may discover our true identity not from any self-analysis but by God's gift of enlightenment.

The spiritual disciplines are ways to truth, stepping stones from our furious activity into God's calm and peace. When we have crossed over on the stepping stones, we escape into the life of grace. Then and there it is the Lord who teaches us. The power of God is leading us. Soon we hardly know where God leaves off and we begin.

Now all formalities are swept aside. Something radically different begins. Something happens uniquely between the Lord and us. Sparks fly. New fires are struck. The chemistry of his identity and ours is felt in ways that seem entirely new.

In my bedroom cupboard I have stashed three boxes that I call my prayer boxes: not unlike a sewing basket with accumulated buttons and bright bits of cloth and thread, they represent a collected treasure trove of things that remind me to pray. Let me describe them and share the contents with you. One is a long flat wooden box (in which, if I am not mistaken, Kron chocolates originally were sent). Another is a Christmas Oreos box, with gold corners and a bright red and green Christmas wreath in the center. The third is an equally homespun affair.

It is not the look of the boxes but the purpose to which I have put them that will possibly interest you. In my prayer boxes I keep things that remind me to pray—reminders to pray for certain people; cards with specific prayers or quotations about prayer worth remembering; small pamphlets with radio messages by people such as Billy Graham on subjects like Christian conversion and prayer; church notices that have meant something special in my prayer life. One such is from the Church of St. John the Evangelist, where I was married, and where, during my years in New York City, I often returned to pray. There is a prayer card in Hebrew called "Special Added Prayer for Airplane Travel," which is really an adaptation of Psalm 139, given to me by my next-door neighbors in New York City: "If I ascend up into the heavens, Thou art there; if I take the wings of the morning and dwell in the uttermost parts of the sea, even there would Thy hand hold me, and Thy right hand lead me." But the prayer has some added modern touches. It goes on to ask the Lord for things specially needed by airplane travelers:

"May you bring forth from your storehouses a propitious wind to carry our plane, and may you sustain and preserve those who fly it, that they may neither weaken nor falter, and may we reach our destination alive and well, without any trouble and injury." The prayer concludes with "Best wishes for a happy landing, Rabbi Jacob Joseph School."

I might find in my prayer boxes a postcard of El Greco's painting *The Purification of the Temple,* acquired on a visit to the Frick Collection in New York, or I might find Salvador Dali's *The Sacrament of the Last Supper,* from the National Gallery of Art in Washington, D.C.

Why mention these random bits and pieces of my prayer life? Possibly to suggest how concrete and particular is the life of prayer. My prayer boxes remind me of something my husband and I had at home when our children were young, a box we called "the cuttings and pastings box." In that box we would put crayons and colored paper, along with leftover gift-wrapping paper. On rainy days, when there was nothing to do, the cuttings and pastings box became a resource for our children's creativity.

Prayer, too, is a form of creative expression that can be both personal and life-transforming. The spiritual person, like the artist striving to celebrate existence, wants to enter completely into the mystery of things.

When we plan our spiritual lives, we are like the architect who conceives of a bridge or a skyscraper and first sketches the design in his or her mind—something large in scope and pleasing in proportion, something to praise the Lord and to please him.

Before the painting begins, the scheme or pattern of our prayer lives may be as modest in scale as a pencil sketch, or as large as Michelangelo's design for the Sistine ceiling. It may be as unaffected as a child's drawing, or as ambitious as John Milton's notebooks and outlines for a grand work he wanted to call *Paradise Lost*.

In earlier centuries, what we might easily call the Great Ages of Prayer, spiritual teachers often suggested a series of steps or ladders toward holiness.

The word used in those far-off times was *perfection*. Prompted by Jesus' invitation to his disciples to become perfect, even as our Heavenly Father is perfect, the ancient prayermasters called us to seek holiness and perfection in our lives.

Today, because of a heightened appreciation for the dangers of perfection*ism*, we use somewhat different language. People who take on the disciplined life are encouraged to seek progress, not perfection. Yet the wisdom of these ancient Christian masters remains as a powerful resource in the spiritual life.

Listen to what C. S. Lewis has to say about what it means to seek Christian perfection. He wants us to understand what a radical transformation God has in store for us. But he also wants us to understand that true perfection will come only at the very end: in our face-to-face meeting with God. Lewis borrows his figure from novelist and poet George MacDonald.

> Imagine yourself as a living house. God comes in to rebuild that house. At first, perhaps, you can understand what he is doing. He is getting the drains right and stopping the leaks in the roof and so on: you knew that those jobs needed doing and so you are not surprised. But presently he starts knocking the house about in a way that hurts abominably and does not seem to make sense.

What on earth is he up to? The explanation is that he is building quite a different house from the one you thought of—throwing out a new wing here, putting on an extra floor there, running up towers, making court-yards. You thought you were going to be made into a decent little cottage: but he is building a palace. He intends to come and live in it himself. The command *Be ye perfect* is not idealistic gas. Nor is it a command to do the impossible. He is going to make us into creatures that can obey that command. The process will be long and in parts very painful; but that is what we are in for. Nothing less. He meant what he said.

Like the Lutheran writer Dietrich Bonhoeffer, Lewis wants us to remember the cost of discipleship. Lewis is always careful to remind us that the Christian path is both hard and easy.

That is why he warned people to count the cost before becoming Christians. "Make no mistake," he says, "if you let me, I will make you perfect. The moment you put yourself in my hands, that is what you are in for. Nothing less, or other, than that. You have free will, and if you choose, you can push me away. But if you do not push me away, understand that I am going to see this job through. Whatever suffering it may cost you . . . whatever it costs Me, I will never rest, nor let you rest, until you are literally perfect, until my Father can say without reservation that He is well pleased with you, as He said He was well pleased with me. This I can do and will do. But I will not do anything less."

And yet—this is the Other and equally important side of it—this Helper who will, in the long run, be satisfied with nothing less than absolute perfection, will also be delighted with the first feeble, stumbling effort you make tomorrow to do the simplest duty. As a great Christian writer (George MacDonald) pointed out, every father is pleased at the baby's first attempt to walk: no father would be satisfied with anything less than a firm, free, manly walk in a grown-up son. In the same way, he said, "God is easy to please, but hard to satisfy."[5]

Encouraged by these words, we can plan a retreat to spend time with the Lord whose love makes demands of us but who is also easily pleased.

JESUS AND PRIVATE PRAYER

Reflect on Jesus as a person of prayer. Bear in mind that Jesus lived, unlike us, in a culture that reinforced prayer. Brought up in a devout Jewish home, he probably took part in formal worship at least three times a day. Everywhere, in ordinary life, the things he did were accompanied by prayer. When he took the bread, he blessed it, he prayed over it. When he went to heal a person, he prayed.

But look again. Even with prayer as the common practice of the culture he lived in, Jesus sought times of quiet, times of solitude. Look at Mark 1:35–37: "In the morning, while it was still very dark, he got up and went out to a deserted place, and there he prayed. And Simon and his companions hunted for him. And when they found him, they said to him, 'Everyone is searching for you.'"

In this instance we see Jesus going apart for prayer, wanting to pray by himself even though he already has a great deal of praying in his daily life. Again, this time in Mark 6:45–46, we read (after the feeding of the five thousand): "Immediately he made his disciples get into the boat and go on ahead to the other side, to Bethsaida, while he dismissed the crowd. After saying farewell to them, he went up onto the mountain to pray."

The same story is told in Matthew 14:23: "After he had dismissed the crowds, he went up the mountain by himself to pray. When evening came, he was there alone." The story follows about the disciples in the boat being tossed by waves, when Jesus came walking to them over the sea.

Then again we read in Luke 5:15–16: "But now more than ever the word about Jesus spread abroad; many crowds would gather to hear him and be cured of their diseases. But he would withdraw to deserted places and pray." Again in Luke 6:12, after the controversy over whether it is all right to heal on the Sabbath, after healing the man with the withered hand, and following the confrontation with the Scribes and the Pharisees: "Now during those days he went out to the mountain to pray; and he spent the night in prayer to God. And when day came, he called his disciples and chose twelve of them, whom he also named apostles . . . "

And again in Luke 9:18: "Once when Jesus was praying alone, with only the disciples near him, he asked them, 'Who do the crowds say that I am?'" Again in Luke 9:28 he goes up onto the mountain to pray; what follows is the experience of the transfiguration.

Aren't these instances encouraging? They seem to invite us and tug at us to enter with Jesus into the life of the spirit, not just in formal prayer but in a spirit of improvisation.

A VIVID EXPERIENCE

I have a vivid memory of spending a day alone in prayer: the first retreat experience I designed for myself. At the time I was working at a high-pressure job, one that demanded long hours and frequent travel, with a high level of hostility in the work-place. The atmosphere was frenzied. In that assignment I felt far away from the spirit of silence and prayerful discipline. Surely I needed, more than at any other time in my life, a chance to be closer to God.

I arranged (this took some courage; it was a bold move for me in those days) to spend a day in prayer at a retreat house on Long Island, out in the countryside about an hour's drive from my home in New York City. It wasn't a planned retreat being offered by some well-known retreat leader. Instead, it was my own day of disciplined prayer. And because it was my day of prayer, I began it as soon as I got up. Early in the morning I went to a service at a nearby church.

While there I heard a reading from 1 Samuel 1, the story of how Hannah prayed in the temple and was taken for a drunken person because she was speaking under her breath. Following the movements of the Spirit in a very impromptu way, I thought, "That will be my text for today. I am praying with that same intensity and beseeching the Lord just as much, and I will be Hannah today, I will take on her way of praying, I will appropriate her style of prayer."

As I drove out of New York City onto the Long Island Expressway, I felt a sense of high excitement and release. I was doing something very freeing. I was giving the Lord a whole day of myself. I was giving myself a whole day with the Lord.

On my way out to the retreat house, I prayed and I sang, using hymns that I knew by heart, hymns that connected me to my childhood: which ones they were, I no longer remember.

But once I had arrived at the country setting of that small retreat center, I opened my Bible again. In the chapel, in the silent hallways, walking the grounds, I moved into Hannah's Song.

My heart exults in Yahweh,
my horn is exalted in my God,
my mouth derides my foes,
for I rejoice in your power of saving. (1 Sam. 2:1, JB)

I *prayed* this canticle very intensely, moving from verse to verse with Hannah, praising God for his mightiness and for his favor to me. In doing this, I learned the great power of these canticles, like Mary's Canticle in Luke. I understood that each one of the canticles in Scripture contains the whole story of God's love for his people. I saw that God's love-story was being re-told to me through my praying of the canticle. And I knew also that I was one with the pray-ers of other times and places, all the holy people who had prayed this canticle before me. I even felt a oneness with those who would come after me in different times and places and find solace in Hannah's Song.

After remaining for as long as I could in this attitude, embracing Hannah's prayer, I came at last to the familiar story of

Samuel's call in the temple. I then heard the words of the Lord as though they were spoken just to me.

> "Samuel! Samuel!" He answered, "Here I am." Then he ran to Eli and said, "Here I am, since you called me." Eli said, "I did not call. Go back and lie down." So he went and lay down. Once again Yahweh called, "Samuel! Samuel!" Samuel got up and went to Eli and said, "Here I am, since you called me." He replied, "I did not call you, my son; go back and lie down." Samuel had as yet no knowledge of Yahweh and the word of Yahweh had not been revealed to him. Once again Yahweh called, the third time. He got up and went to Eli and said, "Here I am, since you called me." Eli then understood that it was Yahweh who was calling the boy, and he said to Samuel, "Go and lie down, and if someone calls say, 'Speak, Yahweh, your servant is listening.'" So Samuel went and lay down in his place. (1 Sam. 3:4–9, JB)

These words entered into my consciousness. They became my word from Yahweh for the day. I was both Hannah and her child. And through me I felt the prophetic message streaming: "He is Yahweh: let him do what he thinks good" (1 Sam. 3:18, JB). I also took comfort in the thought that follows: "Samuel grew up and Yahweh was with him and let no word of his fall to the ground" (1 Sam. 3:19, JB). Later I learned that this story of Hannah in the temple is regarded as the origin of contemplative prayer.

SIMPLE DEFINITIONS

What is a retreat? Spiritual retreat is simply a matter of going into a separate place to seek Christian growth in a disciplined way. Retreat offers us the grace to be ourselves in God's presence without self-consciousness, without masquerade. Retreat provides the chance to be both physically and spiritually refreshed. It is the blessed opportunity to spend time generously in the presence of God. In such a time, God helps us to empty ourselves of cares and anxieties, to be filled up with wisdom that restores us.

   Why should I make a retreat? You should make it because your heart demands it, because a definite yearning calls you to something better, something more. Why should you make a retreat? Because the stirrings of grace are prompting you, because the Lord is inviting you to spend time in the courts of praise.

   When should I make a retreat? When there is no time to do it, that's when you most need to unclutter the calendar and go apart to pray. When the gridlock of your schedule relentlessly forbids it is the time you most need retreat. That is when your heart beats against the prison walls of your enslavement and says, "Yes, Lord, I want to spend time with you."

   Where should I make a retreat? Where the gates of prayer open wide to receive you, where the banquet table is generously spread, in a place of your own choosing, but as if it had been chosen for you: where there's meat and drink in abundance, spiritual meat and drink above all.

   How will I know the way? If you follow the leading-strings of God's grace, by putting one foot in front of the other, your wilderness time will come. This book is meant to offer suggestions, both creative and practical, to help you design for yourself a fruitful wilderness time.

USING THIS BOOK

This book raises and answers practical questions, yet the aim is not practicality as such but rather personal transformation in Christ. Hope of such transformation moves us into a place apart, a time of prayerful separation from daily pressures and cares. Transformation is God's doing—not ours—yet it happens because we choose it, in this instance by going apart for reflection and prayer.

People sometimes suppose that a special reason is needed to justify making a retreat. We assume that a retreat needs to be made on a certain occasion. In fact, no more reason is needed than that your heart longs for greater closeness with God—because you are worn out by many annoyances and worries, and you are seeking the refreshment of God's presence; because you need rest from the anxieties of ordinary living, even from the legitimate responsibilities imposed by family, work, and church; because you want to follow the example of Jesus in going apart to pray.

There are many different ways to make a retreat, but this guide will emphasize the creative process of making a private retreat according to your own design.

The approach will be contemporary, Christian, and biblical, imitating Jesus and his followers and being guided by their clearly established practices of going apart to pray. We also will draw on recent sources, suggesting readings from contemporary as well as ancient writers.

ABOUT RENOVARÉ

RENOVARÉ (a Latin word meaning "to renew") is an infra-church movement committed to the renewal of the Church of Jesus Christ in all her multifaceted expressions. Founded by bestselling author and well-known speaker Richard J. Foster, RENOVARÉ is Christian in commitment, international in scope, and ecumenical in breadth.

Emphasizing the best aspects of six Christian traditions—contemplative, holiness, charismatic, social justice, evangelical, and incarnational—RENOVARÉ offers a balanced vision of spiritual life. But RENOVARÉ does not stop with abstract theories. It promotes a practical strategy for people seeking renewal through small spiritual formation groups; national, regional, and local conferences; one-day seminars; personal and group retreats; and readings from devotional classics that can sustain a long-term commitment to renewal.

Written and edited by people committed to the renewal of the Church, RENOVARÉ Resources for Spiritual Renewal seek to integrate historical, scholarly, and inspirational materials into practical, readable formats. The resources can be used in a variety of settings: small groups, private and organizational retreats, individual devotions, church school classes, and more. All of the materials present a balanced vision of Christian life and faith coupled with a practical strategy for spiritual growth and enrichment.

For more information about RENOVARÉ and its mission, please write: RENOVARÉ, 8 Inverness Drive East, Suite 102, Englewood, CO 80112–5609.

CHAPTER 2

The Disciplined Retreat

From the many spiritual disciplines practiced by the faithful over the centuries, Richard Foster has identified twelve: the inward disciplines of meditation, prayer, fasting, and study; the outward disciplines of simplicity, solitude, submission, and service; and the corporate disciplines of confession, worship, guidance, and celebration.[1] They are a banquet of graced opportunities for those desiring to live the good—that is, the godly—life. Since our enslavement occurs most often at the level of habit, it is at the level of habit that our liberation needs to begin. Two teaching systems influence our choices. The first is cultural and is often summarized in the saying, "The one who dies with the most toys wins." It is a teaching of acquisitiveness. But the teaching rooted in the God of Abraham, Isaac, and Jacob, the God of Sarah, Hannah, and Esther, is a teaching of spiritual detachment. This higher teaching leads us toward the abundant life of God, a life of bounty and beauty, a life of enjoyment and celebration. All twelve disciplines can form us in our experience of retreat. Some, like solitude, we know at a

glance will fit readily into our retreat design. Yet we will include even those that seem un-solitary: the corporate and outward as well as the inward disciplines.

Are the spiritual disciplines difficult? When we take up the
spiritual disciplines in earnest, we rarely find them discouraging. The simple fact of taking up the disciplines is accompanied by the grace to do them. The Lord wants us to come
closer to him and he gives us the needed grace.

Is it hard or easy to love God? I like what C. S. Lewis says
of this: "It is easy to those who do it." The spiritual disciplines
should not be hard work; they should not be a heavy task.
Instead, they should guide us easily into abundance of heart.
The disciplines are our way into the Good Life. They do not
confine but rather liberate.

What is this Good Life? It is not identified with power,
wealth, or status. On the contrary, the Good Life is a life of detachment. This detachment becomes second nature to us when
we practice the disciplined life. The Good Life of detachment
leaves us free to enjoy everything while being possessed and
driven by nothing.

DETACHMENT OF HEART

Detachment means, for the Christian, that we have confidence
in God. We trust God to provide for our basic needs so that we
can carry on his work. Detachment does not mean we will stop
caring about material things; instead, it means that material
things will not rule us. We will have the grace to find what we
really need for sustenance without being concerned about
whether we have enough or whether the next person has more.

"The LORD your God will bless you in all your produce and in all your undertakings, and you shall surely celebrate" (Deut. 16:15). "Consider the lilies of the field; they toil not, neither do they spin; yet Solomon in all his glory was not arrayed like one of these" (Matt. 6:28b–29, KJV). A time of retreat helps us to grow in detachment of heart. It allows us to rely on God more completely and to become more conscious of that reliance.

INNER CONFIDENCE

We also need to rely on God for our place, our role in the scheme of things. Often in the rush and anxiety of today's social life and our sometimes crumbling infrastructures, we may feel dislocated and confused. But the Apostle Paul speaks to us of a spiritual order that includes a proper function or role for everyone. There is room for the apostle, the prophet, the evangelist, the teacher, and all the gifts of the Spirit. Paul in his letters instructs us about the place of husband and wife, parent and child, servant and master. The sense of place Paul speaks about is not the order imposed by secular society. Instead, it is the sense of inner harmony, of knowing ourselves in an easy-going and self-forgiving way that becomes possible through the life of grace. The spiritual disciplines of guidance, submission, and service all have something to do with developing this inner confidence or peace. Verses such as these in Psalm 90 can also reassure us.

Lord, you have been our dwelling place
    in all generations.
Before the mountains were brought forth,
    or ever you had formed the earth and the world,
    from everlasting to everlasting you are God.

You turn us back to dust,
     and say, "Turn back, you mortals."
For a thousand years in your sight
     are like yesterday when it is past,
     or like a watch in the night. (vss. 1–4)

CHANGING INGRAINED ATTITUDES

Still another factor in realizing the Good Life has to do with
the nature of the personality. Certain ingrained attitudes affect
us inwardly. Such negative patterns of thought and feeling
may defeat us again and again. These twisted habits often
come as a surprise to those who believe that Christian life
should automatically set us free. Many people naively under-
estimate the enslavement of sin at the level of our habitual patterns. That is where the work of the Spirit needs to be directed.
We need to invite the power of God to transform us and release us from unhealthy, limiting habits.

This work of gradual change is sometimes called sanctifica-
tion. We may resist this change precisely because we find it
hard to imagine ourselves as saints. But God's desire is to have
us made whole. Healing is his customary way of dealing with
us, and our task is to accept that healing. The Good Life comes
when we stop resisting the invasion of grace.

"The spirit indeed is willing, but the flesh is weak" (Matt.
26:41). With these words our Lord identified Peter's malady.
But Jesus didn't mean to tolerate Peter's condition. He wanted
Peter to be transformed. In the long run, as we know, Peter
was; later in life he was a changed man. Peter's human weak-
nesses—and the transformation that grace effected in him—
should be a source of major encouragement to us. Scripture

gives us vivid hope that "all things are possible with God," even the transformation of our personalities with their deeply ingrained emotional defects.

When we go on retreat, we clear a space for God's action in our calendar. We should not expect instantaneous changes and overnight results, but we should be willing to change. Going on retreat is really a kind of self-gift, showing the willingness to be healed and transformed. This attitude of desire for the life of God, for greater depth of understanding and abundance of heart, is pivotal to the healing of personality.

TRUSTING THE SPIRIT

Making a retreat requires a certain kind of trust. We need to trust the Spirit. In contrast to vacations or holidays in which activities—planned sight-seeing, sports, entertainment, or events—are within our control, retreat leads us into a less predictable situation. We don't know what God has in store for us, but we are willing to risk what we will find out.

I was reminded of this unpredictability once when I was making a retreat in a converted Victorian mansion on a large country estate. The size and grandeur of the retreat house itself reminded me of the palace in the story of Cupid and Psyche, which is actually the Greek legend of Love and the Soul. In this ancient tale (which C. S. Lewis used as the basis for an entire novel), the Soul, Psyche, is a lovely young woman who leaves her home (and her jealous older sisters) and goes to the palace of her unknown suitor. As she moves through the exquisite rooms, she hears beguiling music and finds appetizing foods and comfortable places of rest. At last her lord, Cupid or Love, comes to her tenderly, but asks that she not inquire further about him. He warns her not to reveal his identity to anyone. In fact, he wants to remain a mystery to her.[2]

As I recalled the story I realized that I was reliving it in my encounter with God in this imposing retreat house. I remembered how the Soul is afraid of Love's request for anonymity. She lights a candle to watch him while he sleeps. Love, disappointed in her, rushes away. Many ancient folktales, from Western tradition and throughout the world, speak plainly to our human condition. They often tell us about our fearfulness and failure to trust. They remind us of a loving God who seeks our good but also requires obedience, that is to say, discipline.

When we go on retreat we become open to the retelling of God's fundamental story of love for us, with all its hills and valleys, its dark spaces and sudden glorious surprises. No wonder the voices of childhood break through to us on country paths and in the wilderness of city places. When we take a time apart from the relentless struggles of our lives, a childlike spirit is restored to us, and the lessons of the heart are taught to us again. Through Scripture and story we find out how to listen for God's voice and obey.

When we're seeking to grow in trust we can pray Psalm 91:

You who live in the shelter of the Most High,
    who abide in the shadow of the Almighty,
will say to the LORD, "My refuge and my fortress;
    my God, in whom I trust."
For he will deliver you from the snare of the fowler
    and from the deadly pestilence;
he will cover you with his pinions,
    and under his wings you will find refuge;
    his faithfulness is a shield and buckler. (vss. 1–4)

CHAPTER 3

Retreating Inwardly

Because we are seeking an experience of the inner life, it's logical for our retreat to draw first on the inward disciplines: meditation, prayer, fasting, and study. At first glance, we may suppose that in a time set aside for the purpose it will be easier to practice these. In fact, as we will see, the inward disciplines are not so much a matter of effort as of assent: permitting God's grace to invade our lives and deeply influence us. Each one of these inward disciplines offers a way to experience God present to us. On retreat we have not only more free time but also perhaps more freedom of mind to assent to the disciplined life. Also, as we will see throughout this book, all the disciplines are interconnected and work together for an increase of blessings in our lives.

THE DISCIPLINE OF MEDITATION

Meditation is a form of disciplined attentiveness to God. By this concentrated spiritual activity we open ourselves to the nature of God and to his cleansing grace. Meditation is also a work of the graced imagination. Understand first that imagination is one of God's great gifts to us and has a vital place in the spiritual life. Meditation allows us to put godly imagination into play in such a way that our faith feels more alive. Often this practice allows Scripture to work in us more effectively.

One might choose for meditation some simple story of healing during the ministry of Jesus. Consider a story as brief and pointed as the healing of the man with the withered hand in Mark 3:1–5. When Jesus entered the synagogue he encountered this man. Might you put yourself in the position of this afflicted fellow? Maybe you can become one of the bystanders, waiting to see what Jesus will do. Remember how they watched him so they could criticize? So they could point out how unlawful it was to heal a man on the Sabbath? Couldn't Jesus come back the next day, they seemed to be asking, or the day after that? Possibly, in meditating on the story, you might identify with Jesus himself, hoping to take on his "with my Father all things are possible" frame of mind. Identifying in meditation with Jesus, you might say to the wretched man, "Come forward." Think how long and how habitually this man had been skulking, trying to hide his miserable hand from the rest of the community. But Jesus wants this unfortunate fellow and his withered hand out in the open where they can be seen and made whole.

Now, whatever role you are playing in the situation—whether you are the man, whether you are a bystander, whether you are identifying with Jesus himself—listen to the penetrating question: "Is it lawful to do good or to do harm on the Sabbath, to save life or to kill?" Jesus is asking us, as he always does, to consider what kind of God we are dealing with. Is this a God who wants good for us, who desires our healing and transformation? Just by throwing the bright light of the obvious onto the man with the withered hand, Jesus calls us, the bystanders, the doubters, the accepters of the status quo, onto a higher plane of faith. Had we forgotten what God is like? Had we forgotten how to trust? "But they were silent," the Scripture says. That silence is the rebellion of people who know the answer but refuse to give it. "Jesus looked around at them with anger; he was grieved at their hardness of heart and said to the man, 'Stretch out your hand.' He stretched it out, and his hand was restored." We aren't entirely surprised by the outcome. We knew that Jesus would heal in defiance of the legitimate authorities, despite the wisdom of the age. Through meditation in silence with the power of the graced imagination, a childlike freshness comes. We grasp God's goodness in our lives.

Now meditate on the compassion of Jesus, becoming the man with the withered hand or one of the doubting bystanders. No matter which role you are drawn into, the benefits and blessings of Scripture will come home to you and lead you deeper into the abundant life.

This style of meditation has been a favorite with prayerful people over the centuries. The praying person gains the benefits, the wisdom of the story, no matter which one of the Gospel characters he or she decides to portray. Or we may take another example from the Gospel of John: Jesus at the pool of Bethesda (NRSV: Beth-zatha; other ancient authorities also read Bethsaida, John 5:10–25).

Set the scene in your imagination. Imagine the gate, the five porches, the pool. Now see the people waiting there, some

eager, some listless. Notice what they are wearing, the diseases
that keep them bent over or stranded on their pallets. See them
crowding into the pool, looking to splash into the healing waters. Don't be detached as you look at this. Instead, be present
in the scene. Now you are in Jerusalem for the feast day. You
have come there for a reason. Out of curiosity? Do you yourself have something afflicting you, something that needs healing? Maybe you have heard about the pool at Bethesda. You
want to see how others are being healed. Now notice the sick
man who is spoken of in the Gospel. Go nearer to him, observe
his situation . . . ask him a question. Or ask somebody else,
"Who is that man, what do you suppose his problem is?" Now,
notice that this controversial rabbi, Jesus of Nazareth, has
come into the place. He is causing quite a stir. People are whis-
pering. What are they saying about Jesus? Wait, Jesus is head-
ing toward the sick man, but he is also coming in your
direction. You have to stand aside. Next, listen to the conversation between Jesus and the man who is sick. Jesus asks him
pointedly whether he wants to get well. The man has to *want* a
healing. Then Jesus commands him to get up, to take up his
pallet and walk. The man follows the healer's instruction. He
makes an effort to get up. Now he does get up. Oh, look, he's
walking away. Notice his reaction. What about your own reaction? You have been present at a healing, a miracle. Now Jesus
turns toward you. Are you glad? How are you affected by his
strong personality, by recognizing his authority and healing
power?

This time, speak to Jesus about your own need for healing.
Does he ask you the same question that he asked the sick man
on his pallet: "Do you want to be healed?" Listen carefully. Now
answer his question, but first examine your own heart. Do you

have faith that such healing is possible for you? Do you believe that Jesus of Nazareth has the authority to command you to arise and walk? Conclude the exercise by a quiet, prayerful exchange in your heart with this man Jesus. Call him "Rabbi, Teacher," as his other followers did. Let your own faith in Jesus as healer and master heal your spirit and make you whole.

THE DISCIPLINE OF PRAYER

A time of retreat gives us the chance to reencounter prayer. If we have been inclined to think of prayer as a burden, we can enter into it lightly. If we have thought of prayer as a kind of asking, we can try prayer as listening. If prayer has been rigid and rehearsed, we can make it spontaneous. If prayer has been dull, we can make it adventurous. Praying is really a chance to be creative, like buying a pattern for embroidery or decorating an empty room. With prayer we can take a broad brush, dip it in God's bright colors, and watch our lives become fresh again.

Praying brings us face-to-face with God. Sometimes what we find in that meeting is quite unexpected. A scene in Charlotte Bronte's *Jane Eyre* has the slight but courageous heroine confront a wise old woman who turns out to be her beloved Mr. Rochester in disguise. For me, as for Jane, the search for the beloved invariably leads past stereotypes and disguises to the raw surprises of living; the allure of the Other, the unexpected power and intimacy of God's love.

When we enter into the life of prayer, we are passing through what Jesus called the narrow gate, but we find that we have entered a very large universe. Prayer is really something large and freeing: such an enormous canvas that eventually our whole lives can become prayer. This is the dream of the great prayer-masters and it is not beyond us. Miracles of personal and corporate transformation come true when we are open to God.

People who pray make very strong claims for it. They say it helps them to get in touch with themselves, to solve problems, to experience healing of emotional hurts, to forgive, and to aspire. When we pray, Paul suggests, we stop caring whether we live or die, because we know we are the Lord's. Should we pray for reasons like these? Should we pray to have God's power on our side? The best reason to pray is that God is really there. When we give ourselves up to praying, our unbelief starts to melt. The Lord is no longer a distant someone. The life of the Spirit is not theory but practice. God is not distant but close and loving. God is someone we want to be near.

Let me recommend one of the ways I like to pray. First, I take a biblical text and read it over quietly until a particular phrase invites me to prayer. Then I *live* in that text, I *dwell* in it for the time I am praying: five or fifteen minutes. Now that's the *how;* here's the *what.* What one needs to do (and mind you, this may take some doing) is to stay open. To stay free. In earlier times this way of praying was called *lectio divina.* But no matter what we call it, this way of praying lets the Spirit lead us into and beyond the text into a different space where you or I may need to be.

Prayer is more than beginning, more than the first stab or the first several stabs. Prayer is a matter of keeping at it, a long obedience in the same direction. The rewards will come no other way. Thunderclaps and lightning flashes are very unlikely. It is well to start small and quietly. No reason to tell your friends and acquaintances. No need to plan heroic fasts and all-night vigils. You should have it firm in your mind that the life of devotion is not to impress someone. God doesn't need to be dazzled. God already delights in you.

Success is not the goal. Conquest is not the mentality.

Surrender is the word to keep in mind. The goal is to give yourself away completely, to remember how much the Lord will love you when you fail and try again.

THE DISCIPLINE OF FASTING

Fasting is an ancient practice, and one that plays a special role in our pursuit of the disciplined life. "Fasting," in the words of Dallas Willard, "confirms our utter dependence upon God by finding in him a source of sustenance beyond food."[1] He observes that fasting unto God is also a form of feasting, feasting on God and doing his will. He reminds us that Jesus counseled us in this regard that we do not live by bread alone but are nourished by God's words. Yet fasting seems at odds with modernity, in which consumption is the norm. Jesus said: "Is not life more than food, and the body more than clothing?" (Matt. 6:25). One thing we need to do to experience the blessings of fasting is to practice it not only with food but with other forms of indulgence. Fasting from people, from excessive talk and jabber, from an overload of local and world news, from addictive telephone calls: all these are forms of fasting that can heal and restore our souls. During times of fast I might recommend more reading, especially of a spiritual kind. But not always. In my case, for example, involvement with books and reading can be my source of overload. So I sometimes fast from the pressure of my life by taking a walk *without* pencil, paper, or any other way of recording the experience. Freedom and detachment are the goals.

Going on retreat is of necessity a kind of fast from the pressures of the culture. Retreat is also conducive to fasting in the ordinary sense. It seems easier to partake of a humble diet when we are on retreat. Fewer people will heckle us to eat more, to have an extra helping, to be sure to try the dessert. Our privacy is greater; perhaps we are even anonymous on retreat, or among people who scarcely notice whether we are eating more or less.

Yet we need always remember that what we are fasting from is a legitimate good. The central idea in fasting is to set aside a normal, legitimate life-function for the sake of intense spiritual activity. When the time is right, we will return to these normal functions of life. Paul mentions times of sexual abstinence in marriage as a way of coming to clarity, but this is not the ordinary way of married life; it is a temporary practice for the sake of clearness and freedom.

THE DISCIPLINE OF STUDY

Often we are inclined to think of study as the practice of learning or memorizing in order to pass certain tests or examinations. But the discipline of study is for the sake of deeper understanding. "With all thy getting," Scripture tells us, "get understanding" (Prov. 4:7). Perhaps for our study we should take up an unexpected source of revelation. The natural world would be one source of genuine enlightenment. The study of a tree could become a source of further conversion. Take note of your impressions of the retreat, much the way an environmental writer would. Recording his impressions of the natural scene, the environmental writer Edward Abbey says: "I have striven above all for accuracy, since I believe there is a kind of poetry, even a kind of truth, in simple fact. But the desert is a vast world, an oceanic world, as deep in its ways and complex and various as the sea. Language makes a mighty loose net to go fishing with for simple facts, when facts are infinite. If a man knew enough he could write a whole book about a juniper tree. Not junipers in general but that one particular juniper tree which grows from a ledge of sandstone near the old entrance to Arches National Monument."[2]

In his account of youthful conversion to Christianity in his days as a Harvard undergraduate, theologian Avery Dulles tells of the important role played by a tree. He came out of the Widener Library, weary from reading Augustine's *City of God*, which was an assigned text in philosophy. Wanting to clear his head, he was walking along the Charles River when he happened to notice a young tree just starting to bud. At once he began to discern the tree's obedience. The tree had not invented its own life story. Instead, it was following a path created by a greater being. Suddenly, in a single insight, Dulles grasped the existence and the benevolent nature of God's guiding intelligence. Later that night, for the first time in many years, he knelt to pray. Study, then, implies not only application but also attentiveness: the mind must be prepared to read between the lines of existence, grasping the unstated meaning of every text. Study implies openness to the leading of grace.

Attentive study of Scripture will show us how often the tree serves as a metaphor of faithfulness. In Jeremiah 17 we learn of faith dried out in the desert, and faith thriving beside flowing water. The person of faith is symbolized by a tree.

This is what the LORD says:

"Cursed is the one who trusts in man,
　　who depends on flesh for his strength
　　and whose heart turns away from the LORD.
He will be like a bush in the wastelands;
　　he will not see prosperity when it comes.
He will dwell in the parched places of the desert,
　　in a salt land where no-one lives." (vss. 5–6, NIV)

In contrast to that discouraging picture, Jeremiah goes on:

"But blessed is the man that trusts in the LORD,
　　whose confidence is in him.
He will be like a tree planted by the water
　　that sends out its roots by the stream.
It does not fear when heat comes;
　　its leaves are always green.
It has no worries in a year of drought
　　and never fails to bear fruit." (vss. 7–8, NIV)

Both in the natural world and in the study of Scripture we may find God at work, sharing his life with us. The grace of God is penetrating. It breaks through to us in nature, in Scripture, in works of art and music, in fiction and poetry, in dance. On retreat, our prayerful study of all these riches will be rewarded.

Writing on Retreat

One aspect of study when we are on retreat is in the process of writing. In a book of random reflections by Henri Nouwen,

Seeds of Hope, we learn from him about the power of writing as a tool for spiritual development. "Writing is a process in which we discover what lives in us. The writing itself reveals to us what lives in us. The deepest satisfaction of writing is precisely that it opens up new spaces within us of which we were not aware before we began to write."[3]

Suppose you are in a retreat house in Louisiana. From the dining room, through a plate-glass window, you look out over a grassy meadow. You see an avenue of stately oaks. When you go out for your morning prayer walk, you see honeysuckle in bloom, poking its way up through the underbrush. High above, clinging to the trees, a wisteria vine trails its pale lavender flowers. Capture all this in words. Curl your pen or pencil around the experience. Make little sketches if you can.

When we write, we embark on a kind of heart-journey. Yet we are not sure of the destination. An act of trust is needed. We are often confronting the hidden part of ourselves. We have to be willing to meet the self that surfaces when we write. Writing, then, can be a kind of spiritual exercise.

The blank page confronts us and stares us down. Possibly we are afraid that some distortion or untruth will spoil the page. Maybe we are really afraid of the truth that may mar our self-esteem. But when we override these fears and give the pen or pencil its way, a flow of grace may be felt. Strong feelings or simple insights may spill out. We are in touch with ourselves at a deeper level, moved by the Spirit of God. Nouwen writes, "What I am gradually discovering is that in the writing I come in touch with the Spirit of God within me and experience how I am led to new places."[4]

CHAPTER 4

Retreating Outwardly

What is "outward" about the disciplines of simplicity, solitude, submission, and service? And how do these four disciplines work toward our formation and transformation in times of retreat? Please bear in mind that in practicing any or all of the spiritual disciplines, we are seeking the training of the whole person, a person who even in solitude is not alone but remains in relationship to God and other people. Often it is said of the virtues that if we practice any one, we will experience an increase in all the rest. In like manner, the outward disciplines work in concert to improve and clarify our relationships. The following discussion explores this.

THE DISCIPLINE OF SIMPLICITY

When we go on retreat, taking just a few possessions with us, we practice simplicity. "Therefore do not worry, saying, 'What will we eat?' or 'What will we drink?' or 'What will we wear?'" Jesus instructed his disciples (Matt. 6:31). We should also remember the advice Jesus gave to the disciples when he sent them on the road. "Take no gold, or silver, or copper in your belts, no bag for your journey, or two tunics, or sandals, or a staff" (Matt. 10:9–10). Take simple, comfortable clothes. Take your Bible and any inspiring materials you've gathered just for this retreat. Take a brand-new notebook along with pencils and pens. Leave behind the books you have stacked up to read unless they are really likely to help you spiritually. Be firm about leaving behind your paperwork or other chores. Do remember to take the things that might make it easier to relax: a sun hat, a bathing suit, a pair of broken-in walking shoes, a walking stick if you like to have one when you hike.

One of the ways that we practice detachment and simplicity is by trusting that our needs will be provided for on the retreat. We may have to give up things we're attached to: certain foods, a particular brand of coffee or chocolate, our favorite newspapers. Leaving such things behind for a time is a way of forsaking worldliness. Such things are not bad in themselves, but they are distractions. Simplicity calls for us to put them aside for a little while.

What if a city person, used to electric security systems and double-locked doors, ends up in a retreat center where telephones are few and doors are left unlocked—or have no locks at all? Accepting this practice can be a way of being taught by the Lord. In such a circumstance he may ask us to live without defensive, fearful attitudes, in a simple and trusting manner. Living simply and without defenses for a short span of time is a way of looking forward to the reign of God and welcoming Christ's coming in advance.

One of the ways we can practice simplicity is by doing manual work during the retreat. The retreat house may assign certain tasks to us: making beds, sweeping up, changing linens, pulling up vegetables from the garden, gathering firewood, preparing simple meals. Why should we work on retreat when we have come here for rest and refreshment? The simple work suggested at the retreat house is a counterpoint to the frenzied high-pressure assignments we handle in the world at large. Simple work is a way of coming to quiet and living in the present moment without affectation or guile.

THE DISCIPLINE OF SOLITUDE

There's more to the discipline of solitude than just spending time by yourself. Wilderness time is your chance to detach from the opinions of others, to forgive some people who have made you angry, to come to grips with the way other people are getting in the way of your relationship with God. Matthew 5:23–24 is a helpful guide in this: "So when you are offering your gift at the altar, if you remember that your brother or sister has something against you, leave your gift there before the altar and go; first be reconciled to your brother or sister, and then come and offer your gift."

One of the great possibilities for retreat is hermitage. Time spent alone is a rare opportunity for the spirit. Some retreat houses offer these secluded places, spare and simple, often in places of great natural beauty. While I was writing this book, I was privileged to make a weeklong retreat in the Colorado mountains, where I was able to stay in a hermitage for a time of silence and solitude. From where I was, so high in the mountains, it was natural to pray the Psalm, "I lift up my eyes to the hills—/from where will my help come?/My help comes from the LORD,/who made heaven and earth" (Ps. 121:1–2). If such an opportunity comes to you and the time is right, take it gladly. Be grateful for such a graced opportunity. Solitude also helps us take the beam from our own eye in order to relieve the other person's affliction. "Why do you see the speck in your neighbor's eye, but do not notice the log in your own eye? Or how can you say to your neighbor, 'Friend, let me take out the speck in your eye,' when you yourself do not see the log in your own eye? You hypocrite, first take the log out of your own eye, and then you will see clearly to take the speck out of your neighbor's eye" (Luke 6:41–42).

"All very well," you may say. "I want to have the speck taken out of my eye. But what should I be doing on the retreat in order to clarify my vision?" It might seem logical to use a time of solitude for conscious reflection on the relationships in our lives. But often we do better by drifting through our solitude unselfconsciously, allowing the Spirit to cleanse and enlighten us. What Patricia Hampl says about silence is equally true of solitude:

> Silence speaks, the contemplatives say. But really, I think, silence sorts. An ordering instinct sends people into the hush where the voice can be heard. This is the sorting intelligence. . . . Silence, that inspired dealer, takes the day's deck, the life, all in a crazy heap, lays it out, and plays its flawless hand of solitaire, every card in place. Scoops them up, and does it all over again.[1]

If we consciously give our troubled relationships to God during a time of solitude, we find that, through no conscious work of ours, a new clarity develops. We see our relationships in the light of grace. If we are called to correct others, we will know it, and do it, gracefully.

THE DISCIPLINE OF SUBMISSION

No one goes on retreat in a completely solitary way. In fact, the Christian at prayer is never precisely alone. With us comes a great cloud of witnesses, companions in the spiritual life. John Donne, the English poet and divine, taught us that no one is an island; everyone is a continent, a part of the mainland. The RENOVARÉ vision for spiritual renewal of Christians is based on a spiritual life lived in common, with group accountability as a source of balance and wisdom. Often, however, the issue of submission goes beyond the question of group accountability or group conscience. The whole question of authority may sometimes be at stake in our lives when we are wrestling with questions that affect our marriages, our work, our families, our larger allegiances and loyalties. One text we may rightly bring to this work of reflection: "For just as the body is one and has many members, and all the members of the body, though many, are one body, so it is with Christ. For in the one Spirit we were all baptized into one body—Jews or Greeks, slaves or free—and we were all made to drink of one Spirit." After discussing the interdependency of the body's members, Paul concludes: "Now you are the body of Christ and individually members of it" (1 Cor. 12:12–13, 27).

One way we can practice the discipline of submission when making a retreat is to seek spiritual direction at the retreat house if it is available. Spiritual directors are trained to be open to the work of the Holy Spirit in the lives of those who come to them. They treat our confidences as a sacred trust and they help us to be attentive to the voice of God. Perhaps we have been praying with certain Scriptures, and we hear God's voice insistently prompting us in certain ways. A trained spiritual director can help us to gain perspective on these promptings.

Still another way that we practice the discipline of submission is to come under the authority of the retreat house and its governance. Living its rule, accepting its schedule, we submit ourselves to a graced way of life—meals, reading, common worship, private prayer, recreation, work—all at well-appointed times. Submission to the rule of a religious house shows us, too, the grace of manual labor as a way of unwinding and coming to quiet. Such a form of graced submission may show us again the beauty of Sabbath and the blessing of an ordered life, surrendered into the hands of almighty God.

THE DISCIPLINE OF SERVICE

Often we think of service as going out of our way to do things for other people. Sometimes it is only a matter of serving people when they come to us for help, when they make a definite and concrete appeal. This kind of Christian service is a form of hospitality, of entertaining angels unawares.

In my own life, a person who exemplifies this kind of Christian service is the person who was for me a significant model and teacher of prayer. At a certain time when I was learning about prayer, this person was experiencing a remarkable breakthrough in his own prayer life. He wanted to share the gift. I knew him only as one of the best preachers in our church. All his sermons were clear, simple, and instructive. One in particular opened me up to a life of prayer.

The sermon he gave was about his own experience of making a private retreat. This was a retreat of several days—it may have been as long as a week—in which he was expected to pray all day. The prayerful solitude would be broken only by meals taken in common and by sessions with a spiritual counselor.

When he spoke from the pulpit about this experience, it was a great encouragement to me. He had been a priest and a member of a pastoral team for perhaps twenty years. Yet he felt that in this retreat he prayed in a way he had not done before. He told us this with great humor. He said that when he was told that his retreat would involve many hours of private prayer, his first thought was, "No way!" The slang expression was funny in such a sacred context. Despite the humor, possibly because of it, the sermon touched me deeply. I was moved that a man who had been in God's service for twenty years could move more deeply into his relationship with God through prayer.

When he told others about this, it was, in my view, a form of Christian service. Often we fail to appreciate that we serve others not by taking on extraordinary duties but by fulfilling well the primary vocations of our lives: by rendering good legal services, by doing good social work, by being warm and supportive telephone answerers or receptionists, by writing well. A great deal of work is essentially service. Various forms of secular training exist to heighten our enthusiasm and vitality in such work. Yet there is no greater teacher in our work than the Lord. When we become conscious of his love, we are moved to express that love to others not by consciously setting out to convert others or to serve them in some ostentatious way but rather by quietly serving their needs with a cheerful spirit and a generous heart.

Service and submission may be intimately linked. We notice this, say, at Easter, when our church services commemorate Jesus washing the feet of the disciples. Sometimes we see how hard it is to have our feet washed. Submission is difficult; it is as hard to be served as to serve. Like Peter, we may object, but in our objecting we find ourselves learning once more the cost of discipleship.

Opportunities for practicing the discipline of service may come while we work with others to plan or prepare the retreat or to carry it out (making telephone calls, writing letters, assembling necessary materials, arranging transportation, driving, handling luggage, and other details). Other, less predictable chances for service may burst in on us during times that we had set aside for God. When I am practicing the discipline of silence in times blessed and protected by the retreat house, another retreatant may approach me and ask if I have a moment to talk. When I am seeking solitude, someone may come looking for advice, for change to use the pay phone, to borrow a comb or toothpaste, wanting me to listen to a sad story, or even asking for my prayers. Jesus encountered tiresome interruptions like these all the time. He bore them graciously and responded without apparent irritation. In following him, my task is to welcome the stranger and the unwanted interruption as well: graced opportunities for service.

Each person has a unique way to serve others while on retreat. Often these forms of service are impromptu. Because I am a spiritual writer, I may be asked to guide others in spiritual life while I myself am on retreat. At table, questions may be raised about how I work, how to get started as a writer, what sorts of spiritual books I would recommend. In responding to them I not only serve them but also the whole community of believers.

Retreat time also offers the chance to take stock of the emphasis we put on service in our lives. Has our service to others become another form of overwork? Or is it truly integrated into our lives in a comfortable and valuable way? Have we been selfish in the use of our time? Should we be giving more of ourselves to others than we presently do? The retreat itself is a time to correct ourselves and strike a good balance in our service.

CHAPTER 5

Retreating Corporately

When we take up the disciplined life, we need companions. The spiritual journey is joyful; it should not be made alone. Those who travel the path with us will share the adventure and the hardship. They will pull us up when we slide and relax with us beside refreshing streams. Even the great hermits had spiritual companions! Spiritual formation groups are one very practical and reliable way to join with others in spiritual disciplines. One great blessing of companionship in the spiritual life is easily seen: we ourselves are seldom able to judge the transforming effects of the spiritual life, well lived. By ourselves we become downhearted, discouraged. We need others to help us understand how we are growing, people who understand the spiritual terrain.

How do we accomplish this sense of shared spiritual discipline? Often the spiritual friends we need simply crop up in our lives. They come to us by a kind of grace. And we can pray for spiritual guides and spiritual gatherings, for the graced experience of Christian commitment in common. Such a common faith life is strengthening. It enriches us and makes us whole.

We may go on retreat alone, but our friends are with us in spirit. One way we may honor them while on retreat is by holding them close in prayer. We may also write to them, brief notes to be mailed from the place of retreat. (I have one friend who never seems to write to me except when he goes on retreat!) Still a third way to celebrate our connectedness with others is when we write our retreat journals. We may remember our spiritual companions by naming them in our journals, by reflecting on our friendships with them and the graces that have come to us through their spiritual companionship.

A self-designed retreat may also be a group retreat. I recently took part in such a retreat at a conference center near my home. The group members were from various locales. Some knew each other; most did not. Several of us brought readings and reflections to offer to the group. After a common time of reading and reflection, we went our separate ways to observe a morning of silence. Some stayed indoors in the chapel or in rooms set aside for reading. Others walked outside in the gardens or at a nearby park. At the end of the morning, we gathered again to reflect on God's response to us. In ways like these our retreat became a corporate experience.

THE DISCIPLINE OF CONFESSION

The discipline of confession can easily be thought of as a discipline of reconciliation. It is an activity tending toward forgiveness. By acknowledging a fault or a failure we may forgive another person. We may decide to ask for another's forgiveness. More often we need to forgive ourselves.[1]

Going apart for a time of prayer and reflection gives us an opportunity to confront the failures of the past and to move beyond them. God is never as hard on us as we are on ourselves. Our perfectionist natures penalize us deeply and unfairly. A time of retreat gives us the chance to admit the hell we are putting ourselves through, to relent and clear the slate, to begin again.

A poem by Luci Shaw often helps me come to grips with my own sense of inadequacy. The poem is about broken bridges, but it isn't meant only for architects. It's written for anyone who attempts large-scale ventures of whatever kind and sometimes has to experience defeat.

All these broken bridges—
we have always tried to build them
to each other and
to heaven. Why is it such a
sad surprise when last year's iron-strong
out-thrust organization, this month's
shining project, today's
far-flung silver network of good
resolutions
all answer the future's questions with
rust
and the sharp, ugly jutting
of the unfinished?

Shaw understands our human way of over-reproaching ourselves for our mistakes. She dramatizes these feelings of inadequacy in a passage that reminds me of those lines in the Anglican prayer book about the things we have done that we ought not to have done:

We have miscalculated every time.
Our blueprints are smudged.
We never order enough steel.
Our foundations are shallow as mud.
Our cables fray.
Our superstructure is stuck together
clumsily
with rivets of the wrong size.

We are our own botched bridges.
We were schooled in Babel
and our ambitious soaring
sinks in the sea.

Then she turns our attention away from our own weakness
and toward the Savior's power:

How could we hope to carry your heavy glory?
We cannot even bear the weight
of our own failure.
But you did the unthinkable.
You built
one Bridge to us
solid enough, long
enough, strong enough
to stand all tides for all time,
linking
the unlinkable.[2]

Some Scripture readings may help us also to grasp the biblical roots of our need for reconciliation. Isaiah 59:1–9 tells us

that iniquities have been barriers between our God and us, and these can be removed. Instead of groping like the blind along the wall, we can walk out in the open proud and straight. Romans 3:10–18 reminds us that we are all under the power of sin, only by way of leading us to the remedy. Jeremiah 31:34 tells us that God will forgive his people's iniquity and remember their sin no more. Assurance of forgiveness is offered in Matthew 26:28 and in Ephesians 1:7. In 1 John 1:5–10 we learn that "if we walk in the light as he himself is in the light, we have fellowship with one another and the blood of Jesus his Son cleanses us from all sin" (vs. 7). But if we say that we have no sin, we are deceiving ourselves. We learn that Jesus Christ is our adequate savior, mediator, and advocate in the following verses: 2 Corinthians 6:21, 1 Timothy 2:5, and John 2:1. In Luke 15:11–24 we find a parable of confession and reconciliation. Matthew 16:19 and 18:18 and John 20:23 tell us of God's authority and willingness to forgive.

THE DISCIPLINE OF WORSHIP

What does it mean to worship on retreat? In many instances, the whole experience of retreat will be a kind of worship, a time of praising God and being aware of his lovingkindness to us. Perhaps the most striking form of worship we find on retreat is adoration. In times of silence and quiet we enter into the blazing presence of God. We are caught up into intimacy with him. While walking outdoors, we are conscious of the Lord's presence in the world he lovingly created. We see sunlight reflected on waters and praise him. We are swept up in the language of the Psalms: fields, trees, all living things are worshiping and praising him.

Yet many retreat houses also offer opportunities for formal worship, where guests are invited and encouraged to take part in worship services. Some retreat houses that are houses of contemplation may observe the ancient liturgy of the hours, and retreatants may be invited to pray and worship at those times. If, for one reason or another, no services are planned, groups making a retreat together may wish to design their own worship services.

If you are making a silent retreat, I encourage you to break your silence for special times of worship. At those times the sound of your own voice may seem strange to you, but it will be pleasing to the Lord. You may choose to read one of the Psalms out loud or to follow the services for evening and morning prayer.

THE DISCIPLINE OF GUIDANCE

There are many good ways to understand guidance, but the most fundamental of these is that of bringing the human will into conformity with the will of God. When we make a retreat under any format, whether self-designed or formalized in some retreat setting, the authentic director of the retreat is the Holy Spirit. It is God who provides the guidance that leads us in his ways. When we are on retreat, one danger is that because we are praying alone, we feel we are answerable to no one else. Nothing could be further from the truth. The Spirit of God, his guidance, is felt and known in the joint experience of his community of disciples.

At some retreat houses, trained directors and counselors are available. If several persons are making a retreat together, they may share thoughts and feelings with one another in order to experience the grace of guidance during the retreat.

Often what we experience as a time of dryness or darkness is really an aspect of God's guidance. We are led into what appear to be blind alleys; this is a form of guidance, a strengthening of our will to be conformed to God's will. Hasty judgments should not be made in such circumstances about what God is asking us. We should wait, patiently, for clarity after times of darkness and hiddenness.

One way we may experience God's guidance is literally through the particular circumstances in which we find ourselves (at all times, but especially on retreat). Perhaps the retreat house names its rooms or cabins for people who have done great things in the Christian life. When I stay in a place that is named for a holy person, I experience God's guidance through that connection. Am I staying in a room or a cabin named for Julian of Norwich? Or John Bunyan? I can be led or taught by the special spiritual vision of that person. On the wall I may find framed prayers or sayings of that person. These become part of my prayer. They are also the means by which God guides and leads me.

THE DISCIPLINE OF CELEBRATION

How many of us have thought of celebration as a grace? How many of us have thought that in accepting the grace of celebration, there is work yet to be done? Retreat is in itself one form of celebration. Taking the time, extending our sense of Sabbath in a creative way, is a form of celebration. We are expressing the joy of the Lord in going apart to spend more time with him, to praise his work of creation, to worship him in spirit and in truth. Celebration is not forced but easygoing, with a joy no one can take from us, a joy that comes not from one specific bit of news but from believing the Good News, and believing it with all our heart.

Have we really believed that our mourning is turned into dancing? That there is a time to weep and a time to laugh? Celebration is having a party because the prodigal has returned, and there is no sense in fasting any longer. Celebration is being glad that Jesus is among us, and that he is willing to have table-fellowship with the likes of us.

Taking time to rest in God and to be delighted in his presence is a kind of rejoicing. Psalm 66 encourages us to shout our joy:

Make a joyful noise to God, all the earth;
    sing the glory of his name;
    give to him glorious praise.
Say to God, "How awesome are your deeds!" (vss. 1–3a)

Another psalm for celebration is Psalm 81:

Sing aloud to God our strength;
    shout for joy to the God of Jacob.
Raise a song, sound the tambourine,
    the sweet lyre with the harp.
Blow the trumpet at the new moon,
    at the full moon, on our festal day. (vss. 1–3)

One way to practice the discipline of celebration is to rejoice with all created things. Psalm 148 gives us opportunities to do just that:

Praise him, sun and moon;
    praise him, all you shining stars!
Praise him, you highest heavens,
    and you waters above the heavens!

Mountains and all hills,
    fruit trees and all cedars!
Wild animals and all cattle,
    creeping things and flying birds! (vss. 3–4, 9–10)

As an example of celebration, consider this passage from *Wind River Winter* by Virginia Stem Owens, a journal account of a winter spent deep in the Wyoming wilderness. While much of the book deals with uncertainty, agony, and death, there are bursts of celebration and joy:

> The snow continued through the night, so that this morning, Christmas Eve, the world has a fresh paint job for the festivities. . . . After lunch . . . I take off across Trail Lake by myself . . .
>   A Townsend's solitaire calls to me as I angle among the trees there, a single high piping note of great and pure clarity. . . . Though it is reticent and hides itself, it always calls to the passer-by with that single note like the best-tempered bell struck smartly.
>   I love to hear it call.[3]

Owens is describing a winter that she and her husband, David, spent on a kind of retreat in the Wind River Range of the Rocky Mountains. In much of it they were hemmed in by blizzards and sub-zero temperatures. Yet, in the middle of all this, they entertained guests, sheltered their visiting children, lighted white Christmas candles, and went around in a circle to say what the holiday meant to them. This is a genuine outbreak of the spirit of celebration.

I mentioned earlier that in some retreat centers guests are allowed, or even expected, to take part in preparing and serving meals. Cooking and serving (and eating) a meal can be a celebration in itself. Jesus was well known and much criticized for his enjoyment of eating and drinking. Table-fellowship (often with outcasts) was fundamental to his ministry. He also spent a lot of time celebrating with his disciples. We should follow suit. Some ways to make mealtimes festive are by listening to music, by telling stories, by performance, by serving meals outdoors, or by decorating the table.

Some people might think of celebration as frivolity, idleness, self-indulgence. Viewed in a Christian light, however, celebration is linked to the sudden joyous turn of knowing we are saved, we are loved, and, above all, that the universe and time are in God's hands.

Perhaps our retreat will include some form of festivity, planned by us or by the retreat house as part of its usual custom. A picnic on the hillside by a clear, cold stream is a kind of celebration. A tour of the nearby sights might provide another style of celebration. In whatever form, when we celebrate on retreat, we sharpen our hope for the resurrected life.

❧ CHAPTER 6 ❧

Designing the Retreat

The design of your retreat will begin to take shape from the earliest decisions you make. Do you want to make a retreat alone? Is there a group of friends with whom you have an ongoing friendship? If no such group exists, can you invite a group of friends—in effect, put a group together—for the sake of making a retreat? Who are the people you know with whom you share similar hopes and dreams? After reading the last three chapters on outward, inward, and corporate disciplines, you may have gained a clue. You may think that you especially want to experience simplicity and solitude. If so, you may choose a private retreat. Although some solitude is possible in a group retreat, one point of a group retreat is to benefit from mutuality and shared experience. Even if you go searching for solitude, you'll find that the retreat house is generally filled with people. Solitude is, after all, not a condition of being by yourself but a discipline of attentiveness to God.

CHOOSING A PLACE

A second clue to the emerging shape of your retreat will come when you choose a place for the retreat. No doubt you will find retreat centers near your home; you will be able to get in touch with them by telephone and learn whether they encourage self-guided retreats. Many retreat centers will welcome you, but some offer only scheduled retreats. If you intend to make a self-guided retreat, you will need to know the policy of the retreat house before deciding to go there.

Your church should be able to furnish you with at least a partial listing of good retreat centers. Such centers sometimes advertise in the classifieds of Christian magazines, and there are also retreat center directories that may be of use. Often, geography will be a significant factor: you may yearn for the mountains, the seashore, the desert. Retreat centers in urban settings have a great deal to offer in convenience and affordability for city-dwellers. They also may offer you an opportunity to reflect on urban justice questions and issues of faith in the marketplace.

In seeking the wilderness of prayer, be guided by practicalities. Remember that God makes his presence known in the cities as well as on the mountaintops. Glandion Carney, an eloquent teacher of silence, describes with great beauty a city retreat in Chicago in which he first learned to practice silence. Hearing him tell the story, I could hear his feet crunching on the snow-encrusted sidewalks as he approached the urban retreat center where he went in search of intimacy with God. I felt the bitter cold of the wind-whipped city streets. I felt the warmth of the fire as he entered the friendly parlor of the retreat house. I entered with him into the discipline of silence and solitude, remembering God's nearness to his people in the midst of things as well as in remote monasteries of prayer.

HIGHLIGHTING ONE OF THE DISCIPLINES

You may want to design your retreat around one particular discipline. This need not mean that the others are entirely left out, but rather that one discipline becomes central to your retreat. Bede Griffiths tells how, shortly after he completed his studies at the University of Oxford, he and several friends engaged in an extended fast not only from food but from many conveniences associated with industrialization. In an effort to recapture the simplicity of the past, they lived in a stone cottage without running water or electricity, living on porridge and cheese and vegetables with occasional fresh-laid eggs, and drawing water and carrying it from a well. During this time, which lasted almost a year, they read from many spiritual books, gradually becoming more and more involved in the Gospels. They were young. They were seeking God. This romantic spiritual experiment—which included travel on foot or bicycle over long distances and rough roads—may be appropriate to those who are young and physically fit. But such austerities are not right or necessary for most of us. Shorter fasts may suit us just as well. In attempting any austerities, a wise spiritual counselor should be consulted, one who can advise us in matters of moderation and good health.[1]

Simone Weil, a remarkable twentieth-century woman of prayer, is well known for the intimacy of her friendship with Jesus Christ and the austerities of her prayer life. It is beautiful to read of the encounter she had with the Lord when working as a grape-picker and reciting the Lord's Prayer aloud, phrase by phrase, in Greek. However, Weil's fasting was extreme. Her plan to pray in solidarity with workers and the poor may have damaged her health. Fasting should be undertaken with caution. When we go on retreat, we ought not to be seeking unusual visions, experiences, or consolations, but just trying to draw closer to God. We want to sense his grace and friendship by whatever means he graciously extends.

MAKING A GENERAL INTENTION FOR THE RETREAT

Just as important as choosing a place and a landscape for your retreat is the business of making a general intention. You want to give shape to the question in your heart. A general intention helps to focus the principal longing that you bring to the retreat. Some examples of such a general intention might be: I am looking for a renewal of my vocation; I want to become more aware of my baptismal call; I want to discern my right livelihood (when considering a change of work or careers); I want a deeper understanding of service; I need trust in a time of transition. There can be many such intentions. This general intention or desire is really a rather broad prayer that becomes the foundation of the prayer experience in the retreat. Such an intention should be open enough to leave room for the Lord's work. While we ourselves may enter the retreat preoccupied with a given subject, the Lord may use the retreat to lead us in another direction. We should be open to these promptings, remembering that we are not in charge of the retreat. Everything is in God's hands.

This thematic focus or intention then leads us to choose scriptural material that is relevant to this overall hope or yearning. Scriptures and other material should be planned for reading, meditation, and prayer. Also, plenty of free time should be allowed for rest, relaxation, and recreation.

Here are some thoughts and questions that may be useful in designing your retreat. First, review the traditions around which RENOVARÉ is designed: the contemplative tradition, or prayer-filled life; the holiness tradition, or virtuous life; the charismatic tradition, or spirit-empowered life; the social justice tradition, or the compassionate life; the evangelical tradition, or Word-centered life; the incarnational tradition, or sacramental life. Should you plan the retreat to draw from all these traditions, or is there one in which you particularly want to grow? One should not suppose, because a retreat offers significant time for prayer, that meditation in and of itself is the point of going on retreat. Far from it. If you hope to grow in authenticity, your retreat can concentrate on the virtuous life. The same is true with any of the traditions.

A SENSE OF MISSION

Do you find one particular tradition attractive? Your retreat can be designed and dedicated to that purpose. If you want to work more with the poor or to consider justice questions, you may want to make your retreat in a setting that heightens your awareness of unjust circumstances. Christian groups working in cities often lead tours through the more troubled areas of town, hoping to raise financial or moral support for their work. You might ask to go on such a tour as part of a day set aside for God. Poverty, of course, is not confined to cities, and a drive through certain country places will provide you with sufficient material, more perhaps than a sensitive conscience can bear. In such circumstances you will no doubt begin to wonder, "What can one person do?" Keep in mind that this sense of inadequacy is commonplace and a real prelude to making a personal commitment to social change.

Another way to heighten awareness of economic issues is to spend a retreat day in the busiest possible marketplace environment. Once, when pondering the question of economic power, I spent a day of reflection in lower Manhattan. Not only did I visit the New York Stock Exchange, but I also prayed in the church George Washington frequently attended. I visited Fraunces Tavern, where Washington said farewell to his officers. My intention for the retreat was to grow in an appreciation of the godliness of the American experience and to know how the unique aspects of American power can be turned to good purposes.

OPENNESS TO GOD'S TEACHING POWER IN THE ENVIRONMENT

One of the most important aspects of any retreat is to cultivate openness to God's teaching power in the immediate or present moment. One way we can do this is by being open to the teaching power of the environment in which the retreat is being made. Recently I made a retreat at a center near the Sangre de Cristo mountains in Colorado. The natural beauty of the place was astonishing. Rabbits greeted me on the footpath. Flocks of wild birds flew overhead. Long vistas of trees and clouds and plain stretched my horizons and lifted my heart. Wildflowers blowing on the path reminded me of God's generosity and grace. Even the stones on the path spoke to me in biblical ways: "For he shall give his angels charge over thee, lest thou dash thy foot against a stone." Even as I was in the process of such "dashing," I felt the Lord's providence and concern for me.

One of the surprising and joyful things about this retreat center was the ringing of the bells at certain times of day, calling believers to times of prayer. The clarity and resonance of the bell-ringing spoke of harmony and peace.

FLEXIBILITY IN PLANNING IS DESIRABLE

When designing a retreat for yourself or for a group, the wise course is to be flexible. Here are several different styles of planning, any one of which may result in an excellent retreat experience.

The first style is to plan the retreat before you go, choosing a thematic idea, Scripture passages, and other inspirational readings. Next, draw up a schedule that will allow you to experience the spiritual disciplines, together with rest and recreation. If you plan in advance, be sure to allow generous segments of free time. Advance planning is more successful when you ask the retreat house to send you information on meal planning, worship services, and any other activities such as swimming or hiking. Advance planning should be done in an easygoing frame of mind, leaving room for the work of the Spirit.

A second way of planning is to design the retreat once you are actually on the premises. You may arrive tired, even exhausted. Retreat centers excel at practicing the virtue of hospitality. When you are conducted to your room, you typically find a Bible, selected readings, and a suggested schedule for the following day or week. Responding to the beauty and the spirit of the place, you rest and plan your retreat from these resources and others the retreat house makes available to you: the chapel, the library, the music tapes, the beauty of the outdoors.

Still a third plan is no plan. Openness to the Spirit and a well-disciplined heart are the principal resources for such a course of action. Taking your Bible, your notebook, and your pen, you improvise your retreat, listening to the Spirit and being led by openness, fidelity, and prayer.

In reality, no matter how much planning you do, there will be beautiful surprises. You can never fully anticipate God's gifts to you in the retreat. The creativity you bring to the retreat should be a form of self-offering, not of second-guessing the Lord. There is no way to orchestrate the black-eyed Susans growing wild in the path as you turn the corner with your Bible in hand.

CHAPTER 7

Three Suggested Retreats

Have you already gathered a group together to plan a retreat? Are you considering making a retreat on your own? The following retreat formats and sample retreats may be helpful. You can make these retreats on your own or with a group, adapting them to your needs and adding personal touches wherever you like; or you can use the sample retreats as a guide for the general structure of a retreat in your own planning.

ONE-DAY RETREAT WITH HANNAH AND SAMUEL

General Intention: Renewing One's Call

> First Reading: 1 Samuel 1:1–28
> Second Reading: Hannah's Song, 1 Samuel 2:1–12

If you are making the retreat alone, you might set aside an hour to pray this canticle. Move slowly from one stanza to the next, letting the music of the canticle dwell in your heart. As you move from verse to verse, remember the Lord's might and favor to you. Keep in mind God's power to act in seemingly impossible difficulties.

If several people are making the retreat together, you might want to read the canticle aloud, taking turns with the stanzas. Again, allow an hour for the canticle. But read it together aloud first, then continue praying through the canticle in silence. You may want to separate for this silent prayer time and reconvene at a specified time.

At the end of the prayer time, if you are alone, you may want to record the flow of the morning's thoughts in your journal. If you are in a group, you may want to discuss the experience. The following questions may assist you.

Segment One

1. Have I experienced a predicament in which I felt God was unwilling to act and which I myself was powerless to overcome?

2. What do I need to do to make an act of trust such as Hannah made?

3. How is the Lord responding to my need?

4. Do I sometimes experience misunderstanding when I am acting in good faith?

5. How can I deepen my capacity for prayer?

Segment Two

1. Have I conceived of a big enough God? Am I fully conscious of God's power?

2. Have I expressed sincere gratitude for God's love and protection?

3. Have I allowed myself to feel the joy of God's love?

Segment Three

During the next segment of the retreat, do something refreshing. Take a walk outside if weather permits, experiencing the beauty of the outdoors; listen to a music tape; leaf through a book of beautiful paintings or photographs. As you are doing one or more of these things, consciously dwell with the Lord in the experience. Be grateful for his kindness and favor to you.

Have lunch, following the custom of the house; visit with others if it is appropriate, maintain silence if not.

Segment Four

Third Reading: 1 Samuel 3:1–19

Follow the same practice as with the earlier readings. At the end of this reading, choose one of the following phrases for your prayer.

Here I am, for you called me.
Speak, Lord, for your servant is listening.

Still another verse you might choose for prayer appears in 1 Samuel 2:35a:

I will raise up for myself a faithful priest, who shall do according to what is in my heart and in my mind.

If you choose this verse, you might imagine God addressing these words to you.

THREE-DAY RETREAT WITH THE PROPHETS

General Intention: Hearing God's Voice

It would certainly take more than three days to make an in-depth retreat with the prophets. A prayerful person could easily spend a month with Jeremiah alone. I know one person whose prayer life has been dominated by Hosea. He goes back to him again and again for refreshment and understanding. In this retreat we want to recognize the commonality among all the prophets and choose passages from seven of them that will allow us to get in touch with our own prophetic calls. The seven are: Elijah, Amos, Hosea, Isaiah of Jerusalem, Jeremiah, Ezekiel, and Second Isaiah.[1]

Making a retreat with the prophets is quite different from studying them in a scholarly way. Nevertheless, a few fundamentals are important for anyone who has not done Scripture study before. Bear in mind that the prophets of Israel were principally message-bearers. God spoke to them in the middle of a complex political predicament, asking them to alert the entire society to do his will. This understanding of prophecy is far more crucial than any other dimension, such as seeing the future, or predicting things to come, which are also attributed to the prophets. To prophesy is to speak God's word to the people. And the prophets did not assume this role with any great eagerness. On the contrary, they were often reluctant.

God seized and sent them. He put his word into their mouths. By and large the people who took on this dangerous and uncomfortable role were men. Yet the Scriptures also recognize that women may be called to prophesy.[2]

When you are reading through the selections provided, bear in mind that the Hebrew prophets spoke in the context of a special relationship between the Israelites and Yahweh. Israel was a people covenanted to Yahweh. Today, in our efforts to understand Hebrew-Christian relations in greater clarity, theologians propose many different theories of covenant. Both Christians and Jews perceive themselves as belonging to God's covenant, and there are many discussions and debates about the nature of this covenant experience.

Specifics may vary, but the basics are these: God's covenant is initiated by Yahweh, not by his people. The covenant means to benefit us with protection and prosperity. It is a two-way agreement between God and us. And it promises consequences if people do not fulfill their end of the agreement. God speaks to his people with a demanding love. He asks us to be faithful to him as he is faithful to us.

The retreat is divided into seven segments, with readings from each of the above-mentioned prophets. These segments should be covered over the three days of the retreat but not necessarily in any prescribed order. As you read each group of selections, pause in the place that affects you most and leads you into prayer. Go into a place apart and continue to pray, following God's voice to you as spoken through the prophet. Continue to pray as long as God's voice leads you. Do not interrupt the process of prayer until you feel worn out or in need of food and refreshment. The point of the readings is not to "cover all seven of the prophets" but rather to be led by the prophets into your own response to God's call.

If other stimuli in the retreat setting heighten your imagination—paintings, music, visuals of any kind, books about the experience of the prophets—do not hesitate to integrate these into your prayerful encounter with the prophets.

Record the experience of encountering each prophet in your journal. However, do not feel the obligation to write about the experience until your prayer encounter has ended. Journal-writing should be a tool for the prayerful imagination, not an obligation.

Build variety into each day. Include a balance of quiet time, chapel time, outdoor walks if practical and available, and moments of rest and relaxation.

As you move through the readings for each prophet, you will find that an order of prayer and reflection develops naturally in your encounter with the text. Take that into your next encounter with one of the prophets. Do not be concerned about dividing your time equally among the seven; follow the leading of grace.

At the end of each segment with one of the prophets, reflect in the following manner:

1. How did the prophet speak to me?

2. What might the Lord be saying to me through the prophet?

3. How am I called to act in my contemporary situation through God's inspiration?

4. What might God be saying to his people collectively through my way of acting, speaking, or writing?

Segment One: Elijah

Bear in mind that Elijah's most noticeable quality is his zeal for the work of the Lord.

> 1 Kings 17 and 18 (Elijah's First Mission)
> 1 Kings 21 (Elijah's Second Mission)
> 1 Kings 19
> 2 Kings 2:9–12

Segment Two: Amos

Keep a vision in mind of Amos as a prophet of conversion and justice. He is asking Israel to turn and repent.

> Amos 1:1
> 2 Kings 14:23–29
> Amos 6:1
> Amos 8:4–6
> Amos 5:14
> Amos 5:21–24

Segment Three: Hosea

Hosea's personal story—the unfaithfulness of his wife—becomes the lens through which he sees the unfaithfulness of Israel and understands God's loving forgiveness of her.

All of Hosea can be read through easily, as it is short. For prayer, concentrate on Chapters 11, 12, and 13.

Segment Four: Isaiah of Jerusalem

The first of three prophets known as Isaiah, Isaiah of Jerusalem holds God in awe and is rooted in him alone. He is also known for his expectation of the Messiah in 7:14–16; 9:1–6; and 11:1–9.

> Isaiah 6:1–13 (Story of Isaiah's Call)
> Isaiah 5:1–7 (Core of the Prophetic Message)
> Isaiah 12:1–6 (God's Promise)

Segment Five: Jeremiah

Jeremiah was summoned to prophesy as a young man. He argued with Yahweh about this. He was a prophet in Israel for some forty years.

> Jeremiah 1:7–19 (Jeremiah's Call); also 20:9
> Jeremiah 12:1–4
> Jeremiah 15:15–18
> Jeremiah 20:7–18
> Jeremiah 31:31–34

Segment Six: Ezekiel

Ezekiel was a visionary. His vision of the valley of the dry bones is familiar to most of us through African-American spirituals. Ezekiel, perhaps more than the other prophets, teaches us to trust bizarre emotional events in our lives as means of grace.

Ezekiel 1:1 to 3:16
Ezekiel 37:1–14
Ezekiel 8:1 to 11:13
Ezekiel 40:1 to 44:3
Ezekiel 47:1–12
Ezekiel 11:1
Ezekiel 40:1–2

Segment Seven: Second Isaiah

The beautiful poetry of Second Isaiah (Deutero-Isaiah) is some of the most cherished language in Scripture. Although his real name is not known, he is, like the anonymous author of *The Cloud of Unknowing,* one of our most profound spiritual teachers.

Consider reading Isaiah chapters 40 to 55 in their entirety, then concentrate on specific passages for prayer.

Isaiah 40:3–5
Isaiah 41:18–20
Isaiah 42:1–4
Isaiah 42:15–16
Isaiah 43:1–3a
Isaiah 44:12–17
Isaiah 49:1–3
Isaiah 54:7–8
Isaiah 55:1–3, 12–13

SEVEN-DAY RETREAT WITH MARK'S GOSPEL

General Intention: For a Deeper Understanding of Discipleship

The general plan of the week's retreat is to read the entire gospel of Mark, prayerfully, over the seven-day period.

In doing this, the retreatant enters into the life of Jesus as one of the disciples. Throughout the retreat an identification may be assumed with Peter, John, or another disciple. In order to do this, a certain level of imagination is required when the disciple in question is not mentioned by name in every given text or episode. Alternatively, the retreatant may choose to identify with one of the disciples when that disciple is actually named in a given story. No matter which approach is used, the point of the reading is to take on an attitude of discipleship. Each text is read with the question of discipleship in mind: What does it mean to follow Jesus? What is he asking, or expecting, of his disciples?

The Gospel may be divided as follows:

First Day: Mark 1 and 2
Second Day: Mark 3 and 4
Third Day: Mark 5, 6, 7, and 8 (to 8:26)
Fourth Day: Mark 8:27 to 10:52
Fifth Day: Mark 11:1 to 13:37
Sixth Day: Mark 14:1 to 16:8
Seventh Day: Mark 16:9 to 17+

You will find that as you read and pray through this material each day, you will want to know more about Jesus and the context in which each event or conversation takes place. For clarification, you might use any good commentary on the book of Mark. A useful book about Jesus is Bernard Lee's *The Galilean Jewishness of Jesus,* which situates Jesus within his culture and draws a picture of how he lived within that culture. Bear in mind, however, that the purpose of a Scripture study may differ somewhat from that of a retreat. A book about Jesus that makes him more vivid to you is a good choice for your retreat. Your use of Scripture should also be suited to the devotional intent of your retreat. Your purpose on retreat is to be enriched, edified, and persuaded by the text. You want to pray the text and see where it takes you as a disciple.

At the end of each day's reading, reflect. Try asking yourself questions such as these:

1. How far did I go with Jesus the Galilean today?

2. How did I come to know him better?

3. In what ways is he leading and challenging me?

4. How did he deepen my understanding of faithfulness and discipleship?

5. How did I feel inadequate or afraid?

6. Which disciple did I identify with most today?

7. How am I closer to Jesus? What is he asking of me?

CHAPTER 8

Encouragements

THE GAPS ARE THE THING

Do you remember how Ezekiel chides the false prophets who have not gone up into the gaps?

In *Pilgrim at Tinker Creek,* Annie Dillard has this to say about the Ezekiel text:

> The gaps are the thing. The gaps are the spirit's one home, the altitudes and latitudes so dazzlingly spare and clean that the spirit can discover itself for the first time like a once-blind man unbound. The gaps are the clifts in the rock where you cower to see the back parts of God; they are the fissures between mountains and cells the wind lances through, the icy narrowing fiords splitting the cliffs of mystery. Go up into the gaps. If you can find them; they shift and vanish too. Stalk the gaps. Squeak into a gap in the soil, turn, and unlock—more than a maple—a universe. This is how you spend this

afternoon, and tomorrow morning, and tomorrow afternoon. *Spend* the afternoon. You can't take it with you.[1]

Perhaps the most important gaps are not those in physical mountain ranges but the spiritual gaps, the abyss of our unwillingness to confront the Lord, to come to terms with reality.

Simple, and faithful, and free, we need to spend afternoons (and mornings) wrapped in the presence of the Lord, living and moving and having our being in him. Seeing, now and then, through the veil that separates us from the fullness of life. Waiting, in a spirit of detachment and abandonment, for the coming of the Lord.

GOD'S IMPROVISATION

For us, the most important issue on retreat is not what we do, but what we undo. We put ourselves in God's presence in order to be led. Conventional notions of accomplishment, of getting somewhere, need to be set aside.

Take Psalm 131 as your point of departure: "O LORD, my heart is not lifted up,/my eyes are not raised too high" (vs. 1a). We need to be careful about the expectations we bring to a retreat. In this it is vital to practice detachment. Relaxation and freedom should be our style. Expectations should be neither low nor high, but instead, the work of the retreat should be left in God's hands. Be encouraged. Make the retreat with a light step. Rest and relax. Be at ease. As we read in Teresa of Avila's prayer, "Let nothing affright thee." Have no hard-driving ambitions for what will happen during your time with God. In short, let the Holy Spirit direct the retreat so that the soul becomes, in Jean-Pierre de Caussade's words, "light as a feather."

Sometimes, without our intending it, a certain activity or event surprises us and becomes central to the retreat. Recently, at a country retreat house, I noticed instructions for hiking. The hiker, I was cautioned, must take enough food and water along and must leave a note behind in case of getting lost and needing to be rescued. I did not consider myself able to attempt such a hike. Yet I began to reflect on and consider the meaning of such an experience. Watching others prepare their kit bags for hiking, I was reminded that I was also taking a journey of the spirit to unknown places. Hearing them tell, when they came back, what waterfalls and wildlife they had seen helped me to become conscious of my own discoveries. Soon the metaphor of mountain-climbing took hold of me and spoke to my heart.

About that time I was leafing through a book about the spirituality of John of the Cross. It dawned on me that this remarkable man of prayer had been formed by the notion of a steep ascent to God, a mountain climb toward the Divine. Mount Carmel, a mountain in the Holy Land, was his figure, and that of his fellow contemplatives, for this ascent.

Then I came across this sentence: "Carmel is nothing more than living out in a stark manner the essence of the Christian vocation."[2] I copied this sentence onto a small piece of paper, then broke it into phrases. By folding the paper I was able to take one phrase at a time and use it as a starting point for prayer. For an hour I prayed through this single sentence, dwelling in each phrase. "Carmel . . ." I lingered in the presence of God at the foot of the mountain. "Is nothing more . . ." I let go and began to experience nothing, *nada*, detachment. "In a stark manner . . ." I came closer to God. "The essence of the Christian vocation." God was present, I sensed, at each turning point of the thought. Only with great reluctance was I able to move on from one phrase to the next, so riveting was the vivid immediacy of God's presence in each word or coupling of words. I, too, was climbing the mountain. My ascent into the upper reaches of God's presence came by grace, yet I discovered it by embracing the figure of the mountainous journey, the ascent to Divine Wisdom and Love. Less and less was I conscious of any effort on my part, more and more was I lifted by grace. Delivered from my fretful doing, I was set loose to play in the high places of God.

Such things as these may happen on retreat, but there are no guarantees about how they happen. Everything is God's improvisation, yet we must leave space for such possibilities.

ACCEPT THE INVITATION

What if you are invited, as I was, to spend time in spiritual conversation with one of the soul-guides in your retreat house? A simple *yes* may open a whole vista of consciousness. My soul-friend and I packed a lunch, asked a friendly dog to accompany us, then set out in a four-wheel-drive vehicle for a spot way up the mountain. There we could command a good view of the whole astonishing valley. What an amazing place. God's work was fully evident. Two hours slipped past in conversation about the nature of God and the teaching power of the universe. Again, I was delighted with God's unpredictability and friendliness.

A GLIMPSE OF SOUL-WORK

In the closing hours of the retreat, you may grasp how soul-work changes us. The soul is a vast, rich ground, waiting for

God's seed of life. The parable of the sower gives us some clue as to the soul's fertility. Within the well-disciplined soul is the longing to respond, to create, to develop, to grow. Such a process takes place in quietness and silence, without publicity or fanfare. Fed by the sunlight of God's love, the soul works unselfconsciously toward wholeness. Spirit and soul, we flower in the light of God.

LOVING GOD'S PEOPLE

Whatever the spiritual benefits of our retreat time, we must always remember that these blessings are not only for ourselves but for the sake of the communities we belong to: our families, our circles of friendship, our churches, society at large. When we fail to love enough, to act lovingly to others, it may be because we ourselves feel unloved. The experience of God pours loving energy into us, qualifies us to serve others with charm and delight. We need to focus on the ways we can express that love concretely through initiatives that fulfill the contemplative life, the virtuous life, the spirit-empowered life, the compassionate life, the Word-centered life, and the incarnational life. This is a life of presence that bears witness to God's love for the world.

EXPECTATIONS

Here are some words of expectation for your time of wilderness:

- Remember that Jesus Christ himself is leading you. He is your companion and guide, just ahead of you, encouraging you. He is breaking ground for you. There is nothing to fear.

- Take courage; have fun on the journey. The spiritual life is not supposed to be gloomy. You make your retreat with a high heart and a light step. You dance your way into the kingdom with joy.

- When you meditate, consider the beatitudes. They're supposed to comfort you and make you happy. Revel in the positive power of the Sermon on the Mount. You are blessed when you mourn. You will be comforted. You are pure in heart; you will see God. You are meek; you will inherit the earth. You are blessed when you are persecuted. You are blessed.

- Remember that all the grace of the kingdom is present in this very moment. Take heart. Rejoice.

- Be easy on yourself. Be as kind to you as the Lord himself, who loves you and knows how much you want to take his yoke upon your shoulders.

- Try little, short prayer times. Make them fun and creative.

- Don't try to move mountains. Let the Lord do that!

- Splash into the blessings of frequent Christian prayer; do cartwheels in the Spirit!

- Reduce and trim your expectations. Set aside any notions of conquest or achievement. Concentrate on ideas of comfort and entertain the idea of idleness as a way of being with God.

- Take naps. Lie down in green pastures. Drink in the blessings of Christian rest.

- Please the Lord by pleasing yourself. Arrange the day to suit yourself, and it will delight him. Do what restores and refreshes you; don't try hard over anything.

- Think of your retreat as a time to take it easy, with the easy yoke of Jesus Christ. Clown around in the spirit of Christian hope and happiness.

A MEDITATION FOR RETREAT

A useful attitude for retreat is to offer ourselves as a gift and offering. We need to come before God in a childlike way.

With groups and by myself I have sometimes used the following meditation.

Emilie's Meditation

These days we have set aside for knowing you. It is all we have to give, the only coin we have to spend: ourselves. We know that when we give ourselves, we are only giving back what is already yours. We come to give that gift anyway. For some of us, it is rare to spend even a single day, let alone a week, with you. But we may already know how to visit with you in the cracks and crevices of other days: overscheduled days, pressured days, workdays. Now we have come to make a new effort, a new surrender to the disciplines of the Spirit. We have come to make an effort that is both scheduled and unscheduled: an opportunity, an improvisation. We are in search of a fresh start, a new page. Not that we are complete beginners. Maybe we know too much. Maybe we already know *all about prayer* (but we forget to put our knowledge into practice). Possibly we can talk a good game of prayer, very sophisticated and impressive, like the young Tom Merton at cocktail parties at Columbia University. In those days he knew all about being a Christian, but he wasn't yet living like one. He said he was already dreaming about union with the Lord, but he wasn't even keeping the slightest rudiments of the moral law. We know we could get by with looking good to others. But there's something in us that is a little too honest for that. We don't want to coast on what we know about the spiritual life. We want to pray, to meditate, to be renewed in mind and heart.

We don't want to get by on the praying we did last week, last year. We want the immediacy of this moment, this day, this time with you.

Today, Lord, here I am. I come to be with you. I'm putting all my fakery and false starts behind me. Teach me the way of your statutes, and I will keep them to the end. Set my feet on the path, and I will walk with you. All the rugged way.

Give me the grace to meet you—in a wild, remote retreat house or in more ordinary places. Be with me in parish houses where the chairs scrape and the blackboard whines. When I am in the city and the traffic screeches around me, give me the grace to find you in the noise of things.

Give me the grace to see you in the hard times: in weary times, traffic jams, supermarket lines, unemployment lines; when I am wrestling with major life choices, or when nothing in particular is at stake; when the economic squeeze is on; when I feel myself at the end of the line, give me the grace to find you, even there.

And in the times of my own deep longing: in desolation, emptiness, despair; when trouble piles up; when stress is my daily companion; when I'm not feeling well; when I don't seem to be getting better; when family tensions build up; when I don't know where to turn or what to depend on; let me know you in the whirlwind, Lord; I need you there.

And if my life has no shape to it, no sense of immediate meaning, if I have no feeling of destiny, no vision of my own work, no sense of being called, give me the grace to wait, to know you will make sense of it; even when I can't see it, give me the grace to hold on.

Lord, we are here to be your children: children for your sake. We are too old to be children; we have forgotten how. We have lost the knack of playing, of letting our hearts go up like balloons. Remind us, Lord, of how you want us to be. Let our prayers spring up like clover. Let us be free as dandelions, just today.

You have called us to a new childhood, a childhood of the heart. You have asked us not to worry about what we eat and drink, or what we are going to wear today, or how we will get by. You have told us to stop fretting about how to behave or worrying about what is the correct thing to do or to say. Give us the grace to be children in your presence. Teach us to be lilies who don't have to work at being beautiful. Teach us to be unselfconscious like the birds who depend on you and give glory to you with every rush of wings and every shriek of praise.

And if today we hear your voice speaking in the depths of the heart, never reproaching, always demanding, let us be open to what you ask. Let the wind of grace blow through us.

Scatter the dust of our indifference. Make us open to loving you. Make us generous, Lord; give us the courage to be yours, completely.

Help us to follow you at least as far as Jerusalem. We'll crowd out onto the rooftops. We'll hang from the trees. We'll wave our palm fronds and say, "Blessed is he who comes in the name of the Lord. Hosanna in the highest." And, if it suits you, make us ready to follow you even farther than that.

We know we are weak, Lord. We know the way is hard. And we don't entirely know what you are asking. We know that when our faith is tested, we're likely to crumple up. We're afraid, Lord. But we're holding on. We assume that if you made a saint out of Peter, there must be a little hope for us. So, give out the palms, and we'll walk as far as we can.

Most of all, we ask you to show us the splendor of what you have already given us: life itself, and more than that, life with you.

We ask you to reveal your beauty to us in created things. We ask to see you in things created by women and men. We look for your image breaking through everywhere, not only in stained-glass windows but in the vulnerability of others and in the transparency of loving friends.

We ask you to show us and lead us to simplicity of life and simplicity of heart. Lord, help us to know you in the middle of life, to know you in the breaking of bread, in song, in fellowship, and in the cleansing of our hearts by penitence and prayer.

Give us time in the wilderness for the renewing and restoring of our hearts in the way of Jesus Christ.

In closing, let me offer one last suggestion. Two weeks after your retreat is over, try writing in your journal about the experience. Perhaps more acutely than on the last day of your retreat, you will be able to sense the ways your retreat has changed you. You will see how a closer relationship to God is at work in your day-to-day life.[3]

Texts for Reflection

I have included here some short texts that I collected for reflection during retreat times and other times set aside for reflection and prayer. Perhaps the reader will want to start his or her own collection. They come in handy, as handy as the prayer boxes I mentioned in an earlier chapter. Please feel free to use them during your retreat.

> LORD, you have been our dwelling place
>   in all generations.
> Before the mountains were brought forth,
>   or ever you had formed the earth and the world,
>   from everlasting to everlasting you are God.
>
> You turn us back to dust,
>   and say, "Turn back, you mortals."
> For a thousand years in your sight
>   are like yesterday when it is past,
>   or like a watch in the night. (Ps. 90:1–4)

You who live in the shelter of the Most High,
    who abide in the shadow of the Almighty,
will say to the LORD, "My refuge and my fortress;
    my God, in whom I trust."
For he will deliver you from the snare of the fowler
    and from the deadly pestilence;
he will cover you with his pinions,
    and under his wings you will find refuge;
    his faithfulness is a shield and buckler. (Ps. 91:1–4)

This is what the LORD says:

"Cursed is the one who trusts in man,
    who depends on flesh for his strength
    and whose heart turns away from the LORD.
He will be like a bush in the wastelands;
    He will not see prosperity when it comes.
He will dwell in the parched places of the desert,
    in a salt land where no-one lives.

"But blessed is the man that trusts in the LORD,
    whose confidence is in him.
He will be like a tree planted by the water
    that sends out its roots by the stream.
It does not fear when heat comes;
    its leaves are always green.
It has no worries in a year of drought
    and never fails to bear fruit." (Jer. 17, NIV)

But God is present in reality no matter what unreality our practices and our ponderings imply. He is forever trying to establish communication; forever aware of the wrong directions we are taking and wishing to warn us; forever offering solutions for the problems that baffle us; forever standing at the door of our loneliness, eager to bring us such comradeship as the most intelligent living mortal could not supply; forever clinging to our indifference in the hope that someday our needs, or at least our tragedies will waken us to respond to his advances. The Real Presence is just that, real and life-transforming. Nor are the conditions for the manifestation of his splendors out of the reach of any of us! Here they are; otherness, openness, obedience, obsession.

Albert Edward Day, The Captivating Presence

✤

Father God,

Why is it that I think I must get somewhere, assume some position, be gathered together, or separated apart in the quiet of my study to pray?

Why is it that I feel that I have to go somewhere or do some particular act to find you, reach you, and talk with you?

Your presence is here—in the city—on the busy bus, in the factory, in the cockpit of the airplane, in the hospital—in the patients' rooms, in the intensive care unit, in the waiting room; in the home—at dinner, in the bedroom, in the family room, at my workbench; in the car—in the parking lot, at the stoplight.

Lord, reveal your presence to me everywhere, and help me become more aware of your presence each moment of the day. May your presence fill the nonanswers, empty glances, and lonely times of my life. Amen.

Robert Wood, A Thirty-Day Experiment in Prayer

We obey him right now in everything we can and in everything we know. We take up the prayer of Elizabeth Fry: "O Lord! enable me to be more and more, singly, simply and purely obedient to Thy service."

If we fall down—and we *will* fall down—we get up and seek to obey again. We are forming the habit of obedience, and all habits begin with plenty to slips and falls and false starts. We did not learn to walk overnight. . . . But in time we will see that it is God who inflames our heart with a burning craving for absolute purity. . . . One taste of obedience and we want more.

Richard J. Foster, Prayer: Finding the Heart's True Home

Miss White was old; she lived alone in the big house across the street. She liked having me around. . . . I liked her. [One day] Miss White knelt in her yard while she showed me a magnifying glass. It was a large, strong hand lens. She lifted my hand, holding it very still, fo-

cused a dab of sunshine on my palm. The glowing cres-
cent wobbled, spread, and finally contracted to a point.
It burned; I was burned; I ripped my hand away and ran
home crying. Miss White called after me, sorry, explain-
ing, but I didn't look back.

Even now, I wonder: if I meet God, will he take and
hold my bare hand in his, and focus his eye on my palm,
and kindle that spot and let me burn?

But no. It is I who misunderstood everything and let
everybody down. Miss White, God, I am sorry I ran
from you. I am still running, running, from that knowledge, that eye, that love from which there is no refuge.
For you meant only love, and love, and I felt only fear,
and pain. So once in Israel love came to us incarnate,
stood in the doorway between two worlds, and we were
all afraid.

Annie Dillard, Teaching a Stone to Talk

Throw away thy rod,
Throw away thy wrath;
O my God,
Take the gentle path.
For my heart's desire
Unto thine is bent;
I aspire
To a full consent.
Not a word or look
I affect to own

But by book,
And thy book alone.
Though I fail, I weep;
Though I halt in pace,
Yet I creep
To the throne of grace.
Then let wrath remove;
Love will do the deed;
For with love
Stony hearts will bleed.
Throw away thy rod;
Though man frailties hath,
Thou art God.
Throw away thy wrath.

George Herbert, some stanzas from "Discipline"

One of the most compelling images of the Christian life
is that of the pilgrim, traveling through life towards
God. . . . This is the journey of the heart, which is being
shaped by desire for Christ, our Lord, and its movement
is an upward one.

    This ascent, however, is like that of a helicopter or a
jump jet, which remains horizontal while it ascends. . . . Yet
as long as Christ is our treasure, we are going in the right
direction. [George] Herbert speaks of this as "my crooked
winding ways, wherein I live." But, he corrects himself,
"wherein I die, not live; for life is straight, straight as a line,
and ever tends to Thee." Like the contradictory movements

of desire in the human heart, the horizontal life of the pilgrim is indeed a zig-zag, as George Herbert well knew.

James Houston, The Heart's Desire

Somehow, Jesus, I like praying with a cup of coffee in my hands. I guess the warmth of the cup settles me and speaks to me of the warmth of your love. I hold the cup against my cheek and listen, hushed and still.

I blow on the coffee and drink. O Spirit of God, blow across my little life and let me drink in your great life. Amen.

Richard J. Foster, Prayers from the Heart

Let me tell you about Myrtle, who comes to our house every Christmas and holiday, looking for a little something. Because of some of the twists of the social structure in the South, I have to believe that even though Myrtle comes to our doorway asking for things, she is not precisely a beggar. Myrtle is a person who believes that the promises made to Israel are true. . . . Myrtle is the person the Lord has sent us to be a vivid reminder of God's presence in our midst. . . . Now there is another voice in me that cries out, I am powerless. Myrtle better take care of herself, because I have nothing to give her. Myrtle, for me, is that woman bothering the judge in the middle of the night till he got up and gave her justice. Myrtle is for me, in Hebrew phrase, the *anawim*, the powerless person in the vast, shredding cloth of society, that reminds me I must care.

Emilie Griffin, Homeward Voyage

Prayer does not occur in the heart of a man who thinks God will do it all or who supposes he himself can do nothing. Prayer is a willingness to admit we can do something even if not everything and that, although nothing is done without God, God does nothing without us.

Anthony Padovano, Dawn Without Darkness

"You know what I've always thought?" she asks in a tone of discovery, not smiling at me but at a point beyond. "I've always thought a body would have to be sick and dying before they saw the Lord. . . . and it's been a comfort. . . . But I'll wager it never happens. I'll wager at the very end a body realizes the Lord has already shown himself. That things as they are"—her hand circles in a gesture that gathers clouds and kites and Queenie [the dog] pawing earth over her bone—"just what they've always been, was seeing Him. As for me, I could leave the world with today in my eyes."

Truman Capote, A Christmas Memory

Who has not found the Heaven below
Will fail of it above.
God's residence is next to mine,
His furniture is love.

Emily Dickinson, Collected Poems of Emily Dickinson

A man who works with mentally and physically handi-
capped people said that he asks himself this question at
the end of each day: "How did I experience the presence
of Jesus in the pain of someone today?" And I have also
abandoned the glib notion that all those who believe in
God will experience perfect peace and prosperity. Life is
difficult, no matter how much faith you have. But in the
midst of it there is a Spirit of comfort that cannot be de-
stroyed.

James Bryan Smith, Embracing the Love of God

Further Reading

de Caussade, Jean-Pierre. *The Sacrament of the Present Moment* (San Francisco: HarperSanFrancisco, 1989). This is a translation by Kitty Muggeridge of a work usually known as *Abandonment to Divine Providence*. The translation is fresh, and useful to prayer. Introduction by Richard J. Foster.

Dillard, Annie. *Pilgrim at Tinker Creek* (New York: Harper & Row, 1970) and *Teaching a Stone to Talk* (New York: Harper & Row, 1982). Two poetic meditations in prose written out of the experience of retreat. While the books do not describe retreat precisely, they show how the spirit can fly free in times of solitude and reflection.

Foster, Richard J. *Celebration of Discipline: The Path to Spiritual Growth* (San Francisco: HarperSanFrancisco, 1988). Since its first appearance in the 1970s, this book has been a source of renewed interest in the disciplines among Christians worldwide.

———. *Coming Home: An Invitation to Prayer* (Bloomington, MN: Garborg, 1993). A gift book, drawn from Foster's longer book on prayer.

———. *Freedom of Simplicity* (San Francisco: Harper & Row, 1981). A useful meditation on living the simple life in contemporary society.

————. *Prayer: Finding the Heart's True Home* (San Francisco: HarperSanFrancisco, 1992). A broad-scale appreciation of prayer, with instruction on the practice of it. The book is a heartfelt invitation to pray.

————. *Prayers from the Heart* (San Francisco: HarperSan-Francisco, 1994). Poetic prayers for a variety of occasions.

Foster, Richard J., and James Bryan Smith, co-editors. *Devotional Classics: Selected Readings for Individuals and Groups* (San Francisco: HarperSanFrancisco, 1993)

Foster, Richard J., and Katherine A. Yanni. *Celebrating the Disciplines: A Journal Workbook to Accompany Celebration of Discipline* (San Francisco: HarperSanFrancisco, 1992). A valuable tool for practicing the disciplines..

Griffin, Emilie. *Clinging: The Experience of Prayer* (New York: McCracken, 1994). This reissue comes ten years after first publication. The approach of this book is poetic and descriptive, exploring seven moods or aspects of spiritual life.

————. *Homeward Voyage: Reflections on Life-Changes* (Ann Arbor, MI: Servant Books, 1994). A reflection on getting older, with emphasis on the resurrected life, now and later. Some of the short passages in the book were originally written as meditations. At the end of the book are suggestions about practical steps for a spirituality of getting older.

Hampl, Patricia. *Virgin Time* (New York: Ballantine, 1992). This book, by a poet and prose writer in flight from her religious upbringing, describes a deeply satisfying return to prayer.

Housden, Roger. *Retreat: Time Apart for Silence and Solitude* (San Francisco: HarperSanFrancisco, 1995). This multicultural book explores retreat in non-Christian as well as Christian traditions.

Janzen, Janet Lindeblad, with Richard J. Foster. *Songs for Renewal: A Devotional Guide to the Riches of Our Best-Loved Songs and Hymns* (San Francisco: HarperSanFrancisco, 1995).

L'Engle, Madeleine. *The Crosswicks Journals*. Four books describing L'Engle's very creative and spiritual approach to daily life. The most recent of these is *Two-Part Invention: The Story of a Marriage* (San Francisco: HarperSanFrancisco, 1988). Other titles include *A Circle of Quiet, The Summer of the Great-Grandmother,* and *The Irrational Season.*

Lindbergh, Anne Morrow. *Gift from the Sea* (New York: Pantheon, 1955, 1975). Lindbergh's book is an extended meditation written during a month of solitude at the seashore. She used the time principally to reflect on the meaning of marriage, and found in her environment, shells, sand, sky, and much more inspiring metaphors of her lifelong commitment.

Muto, Susan, and Adrian Van Kamm. *Practicing the Prayer of Presence* (Mineola, NY: Resurrection Press, Rev. Ed. 1993). Susan Muto and Adrian Van Kamm provide ample instruction in the prayer of presence in this helpful volume.

Nouwen, Henri J. M. *The Genesee Diary* (New York: Doubleday, 1976). One of the first books that encouraged me to learn from the monks and apply their spiritual lessons to everyday living.

Peterson, Eugene. *A Long Obedience in the Same Direction* (Downers Grove, IL: InterVarsity, 1980). One of Peterson's many fine encouragements to the spiritual life. I also recommend heartily his Scripture paraphrases in contemporary American style, especially the one entitled *The Psalms* (Downers Grove, IL: InterVarsity, 1987).

Rea, Jana, with Richard J. Foster, *A Spiritual Formation Journal* (San Francisco: HarperSanFrancisco, 1996).

Shaw, Luci. *Life Path: Personal and Spiritual Growth through Journal Writing* (Portland, OR: Multnomah, 1991). An informal and very helpful instruction in the keeping of a spiritual journal, whether on retreat or in the midst of a hectic daily schedule.

Smith, James Bryan. *A Spiritual Formation Workbook: Small Group Resources for Nourishing Christian Growth* (San Francisco: HarperSanFrancisco, 1993).

————. *Embracing the Love of God: The Path and Promise of Christian Life* (San Francisco: HarperSanFrancisco, 1995). A warm invitation to experience God's love.

Wakefield, Dan. *Creating From the Spirit: Living Each Day as a Creative Act* (New York: Ballantine, 1996). A resourceful book on spiritual living twenty-four hours a day.

Willard, Dallas. *The Spirit of the Disciplines: Understanding How God Changes Lives* (San Francisco: HarperSanFrancisco, 1988). A fine book giving the theological underpinnings of the spiritual disciplines, together with much practical wisdom.

Zaleski, Philip. *The Recollected Heart: A Monastic Retreat* (San Francisco: HarperSanFrancisco, 1995).

RENOVARÉ (from the Latin, meaning "to renew") is an infra-church movement committed to the renewal of the Church of Jesus Christ in all her multifaceted expressions. Founded by best-selling author and well-known speaker Richard J. Foster, RENOVARÉ is Christian in commitment, international in scope, and ecumenical in breadth.

Emphasizing the best aspects of six Christian traditions—contemplative, holiness, charismatic, social justice, evangelical, and incarnational—RENOVARÉ offers a balanced vision of spiritual life. But RENOVARÉ does not stop with abstract theories. It promotes a practical strategy for people seeking renewal through small spiritual formation groups; national, regional, and local conferences; one-day seminars; personal and group retreats; and readings from devotional classics that can sustain a long-term commitment to renewal.

Written and edited by people committed to the renewal of the Church, RENOVARÉ Resources for Spiritual Renewal seek to integrate historical, scholarly, and inspirational materials into practical, readable formats. The resources can be used in a variety of settings: small groups, private and organizational retreats, individual devotions, church school classes, and more. All of the materials present a balanced vision of Christian life and faith coupled with a practical strategy for spiritual growth and enrichment.

For more information about RENOVARÉ and its mission, please write: RENOVARÉ, 8 Inverness Drive East, Suite 102, Englewood, CO 80112–5609.

Endnotes

Chapter 1: An Invitation

1. Madeleine L'Engle, *A Circle of Quiet* (New York: Seabury, 1972), 4.

2. Because my first learned prayer addressed the Almighty as "Father-Mother God," I have always been deeply conscious of both the masculine and feminine attributes of God as they appear in sacred Scripture. This volume, however inclusive in its intent, cleaves to traditional biblical usage.

3. John Henry Newman, *Parochial and Plain Sermons* (San Francisco: Ignatius, 1987), 538.

4. Eugene H. Peterson, *The Message* (Colorado Springs, CO: NavPress, 1993), 559–60.

5. C. S. Lewis, *Mere Christianity* (New York: Macmillan, 1960), 174–5.

Chapter 2: The Disciplined Retreat

1. Richard J. Foster, *Celebration of Discipline* (San Francisco: HarperSanFrancisco, 1988).

2. For a fuller discussion of the Cupid and Psyche story as used by C. S. Lewis in his novel *Till We Have Faces*, you might consult Thomas Howard's book *C. S. Lewis: Man of Letters*, chapter 6, "Till We Have Faces: The Uttermost Farthing" (San Francisco: HarperSanFrancisco, 1987).

Chapter 3: Retreating Inwardly

1. Dallas Willard, *The Spirit of the Disciplines* (San Francisco: HarperSanFrancisco, 1988), 166.

2. Edward Abbey, *Desert Solitaire* (New York: Simon & Schuster, 1968), xii.

3. Robert Durbach, ed., *Seeds of Hope: A Henri Nouwen Reader* (New York: Bantam, 1989), 28.

4. Durbach, ed., *Seeds of Hope*, 28.

Chapter 4: Retreating Outwardly

1. Patricia Hampl, *Virgin Time* (New York: Ballantine, 1992), 217–18.

Chapter 5: Retreating Corporately

1. This process is akin to what twelve-step programs call "taking moral inventory." For those who are members of liturgical churches practicing the sacrament of reconciliation, retreat times offer graced opportunities when confessors are available.

2. Luci Shaw, "Step On It," in *Polishing the Petosky Stone* (Wheaton, IL: Harold Shaw, 1990), 100.

3. Virginia Stem Owens, *Wind River Winter* (Grand Rapids, MI: Zondervan, 1987), 118–19.

Chapter 6: Designing the Retreat

1. For a full account of this experience, see chapter 4, "An Experiment in Common Life," in Bede Griffiths, *The Golden String: An Autobiography* (Springfield, IL: Template, 1980), 65–82.

Chapter 7: Three Suggested Retreats

1. The weight of scholarly opinion today would argue for two, possibly even three, distinct voices in Isaiah. Whether or not you hold this view should not prevent you from praying with Isaiah in the retreat. Scholarly discussions and biblical exegesis are not our concern in the retreat, and we need to accept the words and thoughts of Isaiah uncritically. But for those of us who have accepted the different voices of Isaiah, praying with each as a distinct person is helpful. You may choose whatever works best for you.

2. See Exodus 15:20–21; Judges 4:4, 5:2–31; 2 Kings 22:14; 2 Chron. 34:22; Neh. 6:14; Luke 2:36; Acts 2:17; Acts 21:9.

Chapter 8: Encouragements

1. Annie Dillard, *Pilgrim at Tinker Creek* (New York: Harper & Row, 1970), 269.

2. Ruth Burrows, *The Ascent to Love* (Denville, NJ: Dimension Books, 1987), 2.

3. I am indebted to Dallas Willard for this suggestion, and to Jules Glanzer who explained to me how well he had applied it in his own life.

Sources of Texts for Reflection

Capote, Truman. *A Christmas Memory* (New York: Random House, 1989).

Day, Albert Edward. *The Captivating Presence* (Nashville, TN: Parthenon, 1971).

Collected Poems of Emily Dickinson (New York: Avenel, 1982).

Dillard, Annie. *Teaching a Stone to Talk* (New York: HarperCollins, 1988).

Foster, Richard J. *Prayer: Finding the Heart's True Home* (San Francisco: HarperSanFrancisco, 1992).

————. *Prayers from the Heart* (San Francisco: HarperSan-Francisco, 1994).

Griffin, Emilie. *Homeward Voyage: Reflections on Life-Changes* (Ann Arbor, MI: Servant Books, 1994).

Houston, James. *The Heart's Desire* (Colorado Springs, CO: NavPress, 1995).

Padavana, Anthony. *Dawn Without Darkness* (New York: Doubleday, 1982).

Smith, James Bryan. *Embracing the Love of God: The Path and Promise of Christian Life* (San Francisco: HarperSanFrancisco, 1995).

Wood, Robert. *A Thirty-Day Experiment in Prayer* (Nashville, TN: The Upper Room, 1978).

The Works of George Herbert. F. E. Hutchinson, ed. (Oxford: Oxford University Press, 1941).

About the Author

Emilie Griffin has written five books on the spiritual life, including *Turning: Reflections on the Experience of Conversion, Clinging: The Experience of Prayer, Chasing the Kingdom: A Parable of Faith, The Reflective Executive: A Spirituality of Business and Enterprise,* and *Homeward Voyage: Reflections on Life-Changes.* She works as a retreat and workshop leader with Christians of all denominations and is a member of the RENO-VARÉ ministry team. During her long career as an advertising executive, Emilie Griffin has won many awards for creativity. She is a member of the Catholic Commission on Intellectual and Cultural Affairs.

Emilie is married to William Griffin, an authority on C. S. Lewis. They were among the founding members of The Chrysostom Society, a Christian writers' group. The Griffins live in New Orleans, Louisiana, and are the parents of three grown children.

Permissions